Social Intelligence
and
Social Justice

C. Margaret Hall

Social Intelligence and Social Justice *is a guide to discovering the power and complexities of societies and social justice, as well as the impacts they have on our freedom and opportunities. This book is dedicated to readers who want to better themselves, their accomplishments, and the world we live in.*

Table of Contents

Social Intelligence Anchors Social Justice

Social Intelligence
Anchors
Social Justice

I. Objectivity and Social Justice

Social intelligence is social know-how which allows us to be more objective and critical about who we are, what we do with our lives, and what kind of societies we prefer. For example, we become more objective by considering how we act in significant social contexts such as our families, beliefs, social classes, cultures, and societies. These powerful and complex social influences affect how we think, how we invest our emotions, and how we behave. Furthermore, we develop our most meaningful connections, as well as our deepest long-term commitments to others, in the social spheres of families, beliefs, social classes, cultures, and societies.

When we see the broadest perspectives of our lives through families, beliefs, social classes, cultures, and societies we realize more options, especially those which connect us to social justice issues. For example, our increased social awareness—through being socially intelligent—shows us that we are more responsible for our present and future social conditions than we previously thought. In these respects social intelligence helps us to approach and accomplish social justice more effectively than we considered possible.

Understanding families, beliefs, social classes, cultures, and societies draws us toward formulating new meaningful questions about our shared human condition. To what extent do we act freely in our everyday lives? How can we aim for our preferred goals more effectively? Why do so few people consider social justice seriously? How can we become more effective agents of individual and social change in our day-to-day lives?

When we are socially intelligent, we realize that we have a critical degree of individual and social influence over what we do and how we accomplish our goals. We understand that we are social beings, and that increasing our objectivity about our limitations as well as our possibilities helps us to achieve our most cherished dreams. For example, we no longer succumb to social pressures mindlessly, or commit ourselves to essentially worthless causes. Consequently, we are more rooted in those social realities we want to keep or create, and our visions of social possibilities guide us to increase the common good or social justice.

Even though we discover that some degree of social intelligence is necessary for living fully, we understand that social intelligence is more of a means to an end than an end in itself. For example, social intelligence directs us toward social justice, because we need to create meaningful and purposeful goals in order to accomplish our preferred futures, rather than repeat what has gone on before in the past in the present. Thus, in order to better our worlds, social intelligence must be illumined by social justice, which helps us to assess and meet the needs of all rather than serve the strongest vested interests of particular groups in our societies.

When social justice provides the substance of the goals we aim for each day, our good intentions are anchored firmly in social realities rather than fueled by impractical dreams. For example, being concerned about social justice means that we can no longer deny inequalities and unfairness as we assess how we should spend our energies and resources. Therefore, because social intelligence anchors our understanding of the power and complexities of major social influences, we can choose to aim for specific social justice goals to increase the common good.

I. Objectivity and Social Justice

We find that it is worth our while to develop social intelligence, so that we stay fully awake to varied social concerns in local and global conditions. Social intelligence heightens our awareness of social justice issues, and makes us more motivated to accomplish social justice. Furthermore, these motivations gradually prompt us to increase the meaningfulness of our lives, so that we gain peace of mind at the same time that we choose to live more fully through seeking social justice.

At the outset of our explorations about how social intelligence accomplishes social justice, we should take into account the fact that social intelligence can be used for evil purposes as well as productive ends. Therefore, in order to bring about constructive individual and social changes, the emphasis in *Social Intelligence and Social Justice* is exclusively on how social intelligence inspires positive purposes and meanings for bringing about much needed changes in our complex global world. Consequently, we are encouraged to learn about social intelligence as a tool for increasing, not decreasing, social justice.

Broad Perspectives of Social Intelligence

Social intelligence anchors social justice and increases our objectivity because it structures our understanding of ourselves and the world through broad social perspectives. For example, when we are socially intelligent, we consider the varied impacts of the five major social influences of families, beliefs, social classes, cultures, and societies on how we think, make decisions, establish priorities, and make or maintain commitments. At best, our considerations lead us in directions that allow us to formulate visions of a common good and social justice that are realistic as well as universal—we are ethically and pragmatically bound to consider the well-being of all people if we are to survive and be fulfilled.

3

The broad perspectives of social intelligence reflect the power and complexities of the five major social influences of families, beliefs, social classes, cultures, and societies. These social and emotional contexts and pressures support or block our capacities to make decisions for ourselves and others, and it is our responsibility to live as fully as possible by free and enlightened actions which foster general well-being in societies and civilizations. Social justice is a significant aspect of the quality of our lives, whether we realize this or not, so it behooves us to raise questions about what we need to do to increase social justice, by changing how we operate in relation to the social realities of families, beliefs, social classes, cultures, and societies.

Social intelligence cannot be contained by either local or global dimensions of societies and civilizations, because it is manifested in both local and global aspects of families, beliefs, social classes, cultures, and societies. The omnipresence of social or emotional influences makes it imperative to understand the part they play in anchoring social justice in our lived experiences. For example, we need to know the ways of the world in these significant spheres of interaction, in order to be more selective in doing whatever is needed to bring social justice ideals to bear on our everyday lives.

Among all of the five major social influences of families, beliefs, social classes, cultures, and societies, families have the most significant impacts on our emotional dependencies and freedom of action. For example, we are who we are primarily due to how we operate in our closest relationships of the past and present, and this know-how must be used when we assess possibilities to increase social justice.

Our beliefs also frequently dominate our thinking and determine our priorities, because the non-rational aspects of our beliefs are able to take on a life of their own. For example, if we follow blind ambition, we temporarily and sometimes permanently blot out real possibilities for social justice in our lives, because our vested interests over-ride our understanding and appreciation of the common good. Consequently, we can only hope to establish social justice when we replace our bigoted beliefs, because otherwise our judgment is not sound.

Social classes of many varieties—including social classes based on gender, race, ethnicity, and economic resources—frequently blur our visions of possibilities. For example, when we are committed to attaining upward social mobility, we cannot give due consideration to social issues such as how to structure opportunities for all, or how to remove lower social class restrictions that prevent large numbers of people from having acceptable qualities of life in contemporary industrial societies.

Cultures include particular social values and conditions that make social justice possible. For example, social values like equality, inclusiveness, diversity, cooperation, and openness create opportunities for all, and improve existing social conditions which give rise to better shared futures. By concentrating on these new value choices, we not only become more socially intelligent, but also solve difficult social problems and construct satisfactory social conditions more effectively.

Lastly, the broad perspective of societies makes us more objective and more aware of our responsibilities as historical actors. Social intelligence, which in part derives from the consideration of societal influences, makes us alert to the benefits of working with others to accomplish societal goals that have constructive impacts in the present for the future. Our deepened understanding of societies also heightens our appreciation of the importance of increasing the well-being of all, which enhances the physical and moral conditions of members of our populations to establish social justice.

Social Intelligence Dimensions

Social intelligence is our learned capacities to describe and explain our lives in terms of the social conditions that influence us the most: families, beliefs, social classes, cultures, and societies. These five dimensions of social intelligence are frequently non-rational in origins and practices, as well as complex and powerful in their own right. Initially, their influences are expressed as deep-seated habits which limit our actions, but eventually we may choose to use our understanding of them to create and support our most enlightened strategies to change ourselves and the world.

We are born with social intelligence, which makes our socialization possible, especially because we need to understand the complexities of our individual and social lives in order to survive and thrive. We strengthen our capacities to be socially intelligent as we grow and develop, so that as adults we decide either to continue to increase our social intelligence, or to put social intelligence aside. When we do not choose to increase our social intelligence we tend to live intuitively, so that we are either driven by our emotions of the moment, or we follow unquestioningly in others' footsteps.

We temper some of the abstractness of social justice when we focus on social intelligence. For example, we consider social justice in the contexts of our families, beliefs, social classes, cultures, and societies, in order to recognize the social roots of our being and our dependence on others. Focusing on our social intelligence helps us to use personal and collective resources to move forward with our lives, so that we improve social conditions for ourselves and throughout our societies. In so doing, we recognize the deepest aspects of social intelligence—families—as sources of our world views, as well as sources of our calls to action as responsible, socially intelligent historical actors.

These broad social dimensions form the foundations of our social intelligence and expand our horizons, so that we are more objective in considering social justice. For example, we try to see all sides of the social justice issues that confront us, so that we deal with difficult ongoing situations more effectively and more easily. We also recognize our limitations and resistance to change, in order to gain more realistic expectations about how we and others react to significant social shifts like making more constructive value choices, or establishing new priorities.

Families are sources of our emotional dependencies, because we learn many basic patterns of behavior—such as activity or passivity—through our families' interactions. When we get stuck in our life trajectories, we benefit from returning to our families to learn more about our family histories, for example, as well as our own inputs in ongoing family issues. Such a review gradually realigns us with our most meaningful priorities.

Similarly our beliefs, which are often first learned through our family members, are clarified and strengthened by exploring how our social intelligence has been either stunted or developed in our families and varied community settings. Once we know the social sources of our beliefs, we can be more objective about what we need to change about our beliefs, and how to accomplish this, in order to live more fully and increase social justice.

Another major dimension of our social intelligence is our social classes. We start to modify our connections to social classes by exploring ways in which we identify ourselves as belonging to varied social classes defined by economic assets, social connections, race, gender, ethnicity, religion, education, occupation, or ablebodiedness. Seeing the complex bases of existing social classes suggests options for expressing social facts. Importantly, only we can decide which social classes we want to influence, and what we want to do on a daily basis. Furthermore, because social intelligence encourages us to consider possibilities of having societies that are not based on traditional or conventional social classes, we may try to live without analyzing others or without sizing up our social situations in terms of social classes.

The remaining two dimensions of social intelligence—cultures and societies—give us broad pictures of social realities that govern how we operate in interpersonal, community, national, and global relations. We recognize the importance of cultures because of their many contrasts, and because of the cultural meanings associated with shared values, expectations, and ideals. For example, religions have many traditions and variations that create dynamic aspects of our cultures and social intelligence. At the same time, the history of our societies sheds light on how we are influenced and even defined by our societies. Thus our national heritages suggest world views which guide our interactions in both local and global settings.

Links to Social Justice

When we recognize the five dimensions of social intelligence—families, beliefs, social classes, cultures, and societies—we become more objective about our particular social situations. This degree of detachment from our personal relationships allows us to see not only links between these five major social influences and ourselves, but also links among the different dimensions of social intelligence. Consequently, the five dimensions of social intelligence connect us to social justice concerns, because these broad perspectives show us social realities that need to be guided and changed by implementing social justice values.

In these ways, social intelligence anchors social justice in our everyday lives. Although the abstract ideals of social justice mean different things to different people, when we connect social justice to existing social conditions we more reliably choose to take meaningful and effective actions to bring about changes that increase social justice in our unequal societies and our disturbed or warring civilizations. Furthermore, because social intelligence is learned, we can aspire to become more effective in formulating and achieving social justice goals.

Some of our family links to social justice include considering families as advantageous assets not experienced by everyone. One of the most serious inequalities in societies is that some families are more supportive, or have more strength, than others. In this respect we need social policies and social practices that reinforce rather than weaken families in societies. Because families are crucibles for teaching us religious or moral values, social justice and public policies need to help us to cultivate the most durable families possible, so that we can launch members of our youngest generations successfully into societies.

Families are also vital sources of beliefs, even though it is often education that informs us about facts and world views to guide us in developing meaningful careers that contribute to the common good. We need sound beliefs in order to function well in societies, and we benefit from linking beliefs to families and social justice in order to think clearly and make purposeful commitments to increase the common good and social justice. Because beliefs are frequently non-rational, and may impede our individual and social progress, we lessen the likelihood of this happening when we use our socially intelligent fact-finding to guide us to achieve social justice goals.

Social classes maintain social inequalities, whether or not social mobility takes place during people's lifetimes. For example, gaps between the resources of rich and poor people in modern societies have increased rather than diminished social inequalities, so that their conflicting interests usually remain unresolved. However, working toward social justice goals activates our social intelligence to remedy these effects.

As long as we are more objective about our links to social classes, we can collaborate to create alternative ways to organize ourselves in complex, modern societies.

Cultures link us to social justice as well as to social facts. Cultures also promote varied social changes, and are sources of inspiration and innovation for social justice strategies to improve social conditions for all. For example, we understand each other more fully when we espouse particular social values, especially the values of equality, inclusiveness, diversity, cooperation, and openness. By encouraging these constructive aspects of our cultures, we improve social conditions in the present and future, as well as turn our civilizations toward life-enhancing futures rather than social extinction.

When we see these links between four of the five major social influences and social justice, we discover the extent to which social justice is anchored in societies, the fifth major social influence. Contrasting national characteristics of different societies and civilizations show distinctive value preferences and priorities, which sometimes skew societies toward or away from being responsible in supporting their populations in today's conflicted times. For example, when we participate in globalization sufficiently, we recognize that meeting international needs can be a way for rich societies to help poor nations to thrive, rather than means to dominate them.

Chapters II to VI of *Social Intelligence and Social Justice* spell out more of the details involved in seeing and maintaining links among the five dimensions of social intelligence and social justice. In the meantime, the rest of Chapter I explores objectivity in and through social intelligence. For example, because we habitually choose to develop meanings and purposes through our actions, we must pay close attention to understanding strategic social facts as we pursue our social justice goals.

Social Intelligence, Meaning, and Purpose

Social intelligence, meaning, and purpose are only understood fully when they are considered together with social justice. Social intelligence inevitably provides us with varied ways to view the world more objectively, because families, beliefs, social classes, cultures, and societies give us broad pictures of social realities, as well as show us how we live each day. Social intelligence also requires us to make significant value choices at the same time that we participate in our daily business, even though social intelligence does not consistently define our specific value choices clearly. Rather, social intelligence teaches us how to establish meaning and purpose through our unique value choices, without dictating what these value choices should be.

Most importantly, social intelligence helps us to see that both our survival and fulfillment depend on the value choices we make. Consequently, we see that we are responsible for thinking through what we really want our lives and social world to be like. Even though an important social reality is that social intelligence can be used as a force for good or bad, *Social Intelligence and Social Justice* shows us that we are more socially intelligent when we aim to improve societies as well as ourselves, especially because our survival ultimately depends on honoring broad existential imperatives for survival and fulfillment.

Therefore, social justice becomes one of the ways in which we create improved societies, as well as make constructive changes in our own and others' behavior. Social intelligence is unquestioningly a force for good when it is guided by social justice, in the same way that we opt for social justice goals in order to increase meaning and purpose in our everyday lives. Social justice skews our intentions in life-enhancing directions, because our value choices are increasingly consistent with establishing new social conditions which

11

strengthen equality, inclusiveness, diversity, cooperation, and openness.

When we use social intelligence to review what is going on in society due to the major social influences of families, beliefs, social classes, cultures, and societies, we observe that one of the benefits of coming to terms with the power and complexities of these social influences is that we interact with them more meaningfully and more purposefully. When we carefully select which values we choose to guide our lives, we act more deliberately than before we used social intelligence principles to achieve social justice.

In these respects, social justice ideals deepen our fulfillment due to the verve we add to our understanding as we accomplish social justice goals. Besides having goals such as making opportunities available to all in our societies, we have few broad concerns to consider, and markedly fewer new values to cultivate as we create and meet our most preferred goals. Thus, social intelligence makes social justice more realizable, because social justice is necessarily anchored in social facts. At the same time, social justice adds significant meaning and purpose to the social intelligence we have chosen to cultivate and use.

The objectivity we gain, from being socially intelligent, increases our options for expanding social intelligence and social justice. Objectivity inspires us because we see that we have more options than we previously realized, and we are more driven to accomplish our goals due to our motivations to live each day according to social intelligence principles. Ultimately, however, the enlightenment of social justice is necessary to guide us in all aspects of whatever we choose to do in relation to our families, communities, societies, and globalization.

Whether we focus on social justice in our families, beliefs, social classes, cultures, and societies or not, social intelligence gives us practical and reliable principles that help us to accomplish goals that improve local and global social conditions. Furthermore, we increase our social intelligence when we are more objective about families, beliefs, social classes, cultures, and societies. We discover that it is worthwhile to invest time and effort to strengthen our meaning and purpose, by considering social justice in these important social spheres. If we do not anchor social ideals such as social justice in social facts through our individual or collective efforts, our actions may not be sufficiently consolidated in desired directions, with the result that we risk losing rather than gaining meaning and purpose in accomplishing our goals.

Social Facts and Social Justice

Social intelligence derives from social facts, which makes social intelligence a particularly valuable social skill and social strategy to cultivate. For example, we become who we are because we continually experience social realities and social influences. Furthermore, we need to learn what is more or less predictable in our everyday worlds, in order to launch ourselves successfully into societies and social justice concerns.

The dependability and predictability of social influences—particularly the five major social influences of families, beliefs, social classes, cultures, and societies— teaches us that we are connected to many other people, as well as to our past and present patterned interactions. We are who we are not merely due to ourselves, but as consequences of our social exchanges with others, and because of the social facts that define our particular situations.

In order to clarify the power and complexities of the multitudes of social facts that impact our lives, including our decision-making and commitments, we benefit from examining dominant stressors in each of the five major influences of families, beliefs, social classes, cultures, and societies. For example, the emotional intensity of our families as well as the significance of early childhood socialization, indicate that families have formative effects on how we experience ourselves, others, communities, societies, and the world. As children we were strongly encouraged to see vital aspects of social realities in similar ways to our closest relatives. Thus, emotional dependencies in families need to be acknowledged and understood through socially intelligent explorations, especially about who we are and what we do on a daily basis in relation to our families.

Similarly, our beliefs are significant foundations of how we perceive and understand ourselves and others. Beliefs are powerful due to their deep, longstanding influences on our thinking, as well as their emotional content, which raise social issues about dominance and childhood adaptations in our families. Even though we are adults now, some of our earliest beliefs may seem to continue to be integral parts of our physiology, which means that they are extremely difficult to change. However, as socially intelligent adults, we need to make sure that our beliefs are not destructive to ourselves or others, and do not hinder us in contributing to the common good.

Sometimes we blur distinctions between social facts and beliefs, with the result that our beliefs tend to distort our understanding of social justice, as well as our capacities to accomplish social justice. For example, we may come to believe, or at least acknowledge, that some social facts about social classes show that inequalities in social classes are intrinsically necessary to societies. By contrast, social intelligence allows us to be more objective and critical about the social conditions and consequences of social classes, so that we more deliberately choose to devote our attention to constructing wiser ways to organize our populations and personal lives.

I. Objectivity and Social Justice

To the extent that we value social justice, we are necessarily critical about the power and complexities of our cultures, so that we uphold new value choices. For example, we honor the beneficial social significance of equality, inclusiveness, diversity, cooperation, and openness. These social justice values link our cultures more closely to social justice, and social facts show us that when we persist in establishing social conditions that reflect equality, inclusiveness, diversity, cooperation, and openness, we increase social justice in our societies, in spite of the persistence of strong conventional values such as status differences, social inequalities, and vested interests. Social facts convince us that cultural ideals can be decisive positive influences, with the result that social justice may thrive as a more focused direction and purpose for improved present and future societies.

Because social facts include contemporary and historical information about societies, they help us to be more objective in our understanding and applications of social justice. For example, once we realize that we cannot be effective agents of social change without seriously considering social facts about societies, we assume tasks that will increase our social intelligence. For example, we research what social justice means, and how we can maintain widespread social conditions that benefit all, rather than the privileged few, in different societies.

Collecting social facts about families, beliefs, social classes, cultures, and societies enables us to increase social justice more pragmatically. Social facts also help us to make social justice a stronger social ideal to guide our interactions with others, as well as our formulations of socially intelligent goals. We are more effective historical actors whenever we account for social facts, especially when we strive to achieve abstract, idealistic goals such as social justice. Consequently, social facts anchor social justice in socially intelligent strategies that better societies through improving social conditions for all.

Social Justice Anchors

Social justice anchors social intelligence differently from how social intelligence anchors social justice. For example, social intelligence provides social justice with critical dimensions of social realities, by emphasizing the social facts that underlie social situations and social justice ideals. Social justice also usefully reinforces and transcends individual and collective efforts to improve social conditions in societies. Social justice not only inspires socially intelligent interventions, but provides social ideals that motivate practical, attainable goals to better our present and future societies. Thus, much as we need social intelligence to guide our social justice beliefs and actions, we at the same time depend on social justice to make our socially intelligent world views more purposeful.

The reciprocal and complementary roles of social justice and social intelligence show us how learning about social intelligence leads to achieving social justice goals. Our actions make us realize that without social intelligence, our efforts to accomplish social justice are often unproductive. Furthermore, without social justice, social intelligence is merely a reliable means which has no particular ends. Consequently, social justice anchors our socially intelligent efforts to increase the common good, because it strengthens our shared meanings, goals, and accomplishments.

The reciprocity between social intelligence and social justice exists in part because social intelligence reveals social injustices. For example, when we examine the power and complexities of the five major social influences of families, beliefs, social classes, cultures, and societies, we find that inequalities pervade these social spheres. We see that social conditions of isolation, meaninglessness, normlessness, powerlessness, and self-estrangement exist due to these five major social influences. Furthermore, because socially intelligent know-how about societies suggests ways to improve qualities of life, we find that we can use social intelligence principles to make constructive changes in the status quo.

Similarly, social justice anchors our interest and willingness to change societies through improving social conditions, by orienting our efforts toward long term constructive patterns of organization in our societies and civilizations. For example, we focus on reconstructing problematic aspects of families, beliefs, social classes, and societies by making new value choices which are prompted by social intelligence and inspired by social justice. We aim to demonstrate equality, inclusiveness, diversity, cooperation, and openness as constructive conditions and qualities of social life, so that social intelligence ultimately guides us to achieve social justice goals.

We maintain our objectivity, and therefore our freedom, to make varied value choices when we consider both social intelligence and social justice. For example, when we want to change patterns of unfairness in our families, we gather social facts about our families, so that we recognize more clearly who is dominating whom in these intense emotional systems. Gathering social facts, and the clarity they provide, increases our motivation to accomplish social justice concerns, which eventually balances family and social exchanges more effectively in their routine patterns of interaction.

When we use social intelligence to anchor our beliefs, by recognizing how some of our beliefs fall short in their effectiveness because they are not based on social facts, we become more aligned with social justice goals. Social facts explain some of our weaknesses and incapacities to reach our social justice goals, and help us choose new ways to make our ideals more productive.

Thus, the social facts of inequalities related to social classes are indisputable. Social intelligence makes us more aware of what our options are in closing some of the gaps between people who are poor and wealthy in our populations. At the same time, social justice is a strong motivating force for persisting in developing the social policies needed to adjust these imbalances in resources.

Socially intelligent strategies guide us in understanding our cultures more fully, so that we are more inspired to make new value choices that bring equality, inclusiveness, diversity, cooperation, and openness into our cultures more decisively. Therefore, although we need social intelligence to see the scope of our cultural problems, we need social justice to carry out programs of reform based on new value choices.

When we use social intelligence to understand societies, we find links between social facts and histories. For example, the degree of objectivity and breadth of perspectives we cultivate through social intelligence, allow us to understand social problems more fully. Consequently, social justice inspires our socially intelligent efforts to gradually create more meaningful societies.

II. Families and Social Justice

It may surprise us to realize that some of our earliest recollections about our families include our family members' reactions to social justice issues. For example, the pain of sibling rivalry is seared into our hearts as the unjustified neglect of a parent; we suffered from being prevented from doing particular things because our parents did not consider them appropriate for someone of our ages; we felt unjustly treated if a parent left us for another partner when we were young and desperately dependent; and the frustration of being teased unfairly by cousins as we approached adolescence proved extraordinarily difficult to bear. When we feel unloved in varied situations, we often react by blaming a relative for some real or imagined injustices related to our age, sex, gender, or family closeness.

Sometimes, however, these painful personal disasters may merely be sticking points in the everyday press of family interactions, that otherwise essentially focus on meeting basic family needs. Nevertheless, because of the emotional intensity of families, such episodes seem to be critically important in defining who we are, and in establishing our understanding of right and wrong. From a socially intelligent perspective, whatever problems emerge from patterns of family interaction, the fact is that our families are usually the first groups of people who impact us, so at best we are indebted to them for making us human and for giving us intellectual tools to distinguish right from wrong, as well as for our physical survival.

Families do not last unless they have a workable degree of emotional intensity, and make distinctions between what family members believe is right or wrong. There are no predictable or inviolable differences in how families define right and wrong, because they must make moral distinctions about everyday exchanges in order to survive in the world. Consequently, the common denominator among families is that although they are crucibles that distinguish between what they think is right or wrong, it is our own family members who decide how to do this. Because of the clear moral factor in family judgments, we may conclude that social justice is a significant theme of family communications and family interactions in many diverse situations.

Family members are often connected to each other by moral issues, and social justice themes are passed down through time among members of different generations. We not only learn about moral issues in our families through our parents, but also through our grandparents and other members of past generations. In fact, all participants in the same family emotional systems establish their positions by articulating values which show their conformity or deviations with respect to their family cultures.

We are first launched into societies by our parents, and later we re-launch ourselves into new areas of interest and concern as mature adults. For example, we are essentially compelled to continue negotiating who we are and what we want to accomplish throughout our life-spans. When we are socially intelligent adults, we assume additional responsibilities as historical actors, whereby we choose to accomplish missions that directly increase the common good and social justice: we examine the sum total of our experiences, and decide what we can or cannot do to make the world a better place in the present for the future. Even though our own new goals may be different from those that our parents wanted for us, ideally we are now inspired to accomplish them through social intelligence, the common good, and social justice.

When we connect our family experiences to social justice issues, we make more thoughtful decisions about how to meet our family responsibilities before we go into the world as historical actors. For example, we use social intelligence to guide us, so that we meet our family responsibilities by responding to family members' real needs, in order to devote additional energies to increasing the common good and social justice. We act responsibly in our families, so that we can commit ourselves to achieving social justice in broader social spheres.

As our social intelligence matures, we inevitably deal with family conflicts and losses. We benefit from learning a great deal about ourselves and our families as we cope with family tensions, and we often become more empathic, effective leaders in our families, communities, and societies. These strengthened social intelligence skills enable us to live fully, and we give back to others some of the social advantages we already have.

Emotional Systems

Families are intense emotional systems which frequently react rather than interact according to well thought out plans or strategies. Unfortunately, when we are emotionally reactive, we cannot be sufficiently objective to be fair to others. For example, we tend to be driven by our own vested interests rather than support the well-being of whole families or groups. Consequently, members of reactive family emotional systems often do not fare well in developing their life courses, or in finding appropriate opportunities to enhance their potentials.

Ideally, and to the extent that family members develop some objectivity about their emotional attachments and preferences, families are able to meet their immediate needs to survive adequately, as well as accomplish some long term goals for fulfillment and satisfaction. These family members take care of their day-to-day business effectively, and their children usually become thoughtful and productive citizens. In addition, the interests of social justice and the need to provide a viable common good for all are best served. Thus, social intelligence helps us to think clearly, and assess our alternatives carefully, in order to cooperate with others to improve societies for the present and future.

When we are socially intelligent, we realize that we form foundations for our social intelligence through our families, and that we need to return to our families from time to time to learn more about their distinctive emotional qualities and social adaptations. Social intelligence helps us to adjust our behavior, so that we interact more effectively with others when we are under pressure. For example, we realize that our views of societies may be distorted and disconnected from social realities because of the intensity of our family dependencies. By contrast, being free, autonomous, and independent in our families makes us stronger to withstand others' pressures in diverse social settings.

In addition to acknowledging the fact that the original sources of our ideas about ourselves, our communities, and our societies flow from our families' interpretations of social realities, we need to do sufficient research to confirm what we believe about social facts and social conditions in our societies. This prepares us to choose a quest or mission to accomplish that does not merely conform to family dictates. Deviating from other family members' expectations makes us more authentic historical actors who have socially intelligent ideas and motives.

Thus, our efforts to be strong in our everyday ventures are reinforced by our know-how about family emotional systems. We see how non-rational behavior, for example, derails our best intentions, so that we may not be able to accomplish what we want to do with our lives. By contrast, interacting in our families' emotional systems strengthens our capacities to deal with our own and others' reactivity. Because we are not immune to family or social pressures to conform, we acknowledge that it takes determined trial and error efforts to do what we believe in the most.

Social justice issues call into play complex aspects of our maturity or immaturity. For example, we cannot advance far in developing our social intelligence when we are unable to think clearly, or are not able to articulate viable visions of improved social conditions. Furthermore, if we want to make worthwhile contributions to social justice, we must know how emotional systems operate. This enables us to safeguard our quests to work alone or with others to create specific social justice improvements in societies, such as providing more educational opportunities for disadvantaged members of our populations.

Social intelligence gives us tools to understand the emotional systems of families and social groups sufficiently, so that we predict more accurately how to deal successfully with controversial social justice issues. When we understand why and how individuals and groups react negatively to our plans, for example, we are more likely to be able to transcend their resistance to our efforts to bring about meaningful changes. Social intelligence teaches us to keep our cool in difficult social and political situations, so that the real business of the day is done.

Our knowledge of families' emotional systems and other emotional systems helps us to discern how to accomplish our goals effectively in the long run. We clarify our most significant concerns about social justice issues, for example, without getting sidetracked by unrelated or minor issues for a lifetime. Social intelligence supports social justice because it relies on objectivity and social facts, and the solidity of this strength helps us to transcend initial and later disappointments in bringing about increased social justice.

Multigenerational Realities

One reason that families have such deep impacts on who we are and what we do is that our extended kin are made up of people from at least three generations. The fact that we are connected to family members who go back in time for countless generations makes us consider family histories and their connections to families in evolution. For example, recent human genome research shows us that human blood characteristics can be traced to times before historical records began, which reminds us that our genetic and biological origins are set deeply in the distant past.

A brief sketch of multigenerational realities only roughly maps out a few essential characteristics and impacts of past generations. For example, we do not usually consider that older generations of our families affect our lives beyond the last three or four past generations. Furthermore, recent developments in knowledge about deceased generations, as well as experiencing longer life-spans, have not necessarily brought us closer to generations from the distant past. Rather, they have emphasized vast cultural contrasts among different generations.

To the extent that we understand that there are some important similarities among families—such as the omnipresence of family emotional systems—we can infer that the power of multigenerational influences may be considerable in relation to the life outcomes of members of current generations. Families are important not just because they are the most intense emotional systems in which most people participate, but because family memberships are open-ended and cross at least several generations of their most recent past.

Social intelligence encourages us to maintain a multigenerational perspective in understanding our own families and families in societies. Multigenerational exchanges are the longest lasting behavior patterns of family members from the past, which predictably make differences to our life chances and opportunities throughout our lives. For example, we may be integral parts of successfully adaptive multigenerational patterns of family interaction, or we may be members of continuing family dysfunctions over several generations. Repeating family dysfunctions is not inevitable, but we need to be aware of this particular impact on our behavior, as well as the five major social influences of families, beliefs, social classes, cultures, and societies.

Multigenerational perspectives and realities are forces to be reckoned with when we try to build social intelligence. As in the case of other broad social perspectives, such as beliefs, we learn more about societies and ourselves when we consider the power and complexities of multigenerational influences within and among families. Repeated patterns of behavior throughout different generations of the same families have inescapable effects on members of the youngest generations, especially when repeated patterns of behavior— such as political involvement—are sufficiently clear to understand and observe during the lifetimes of these young family members.

Whatever families' postures are toward social issues such as social justice, repeated behavior across several generations often predisposes us to act similarly. Although multigenerational repeats are not hereditary, we are likely to repeat some of the same patterns of behavior without question, or feel compelled to meet family expectations to act like members of our past generations. For example, many families deliberately train their children to follow in the footsteps of successful family members, or sometimes their children choose to repeat undesirable behavior in past generations. These influences are strong and compelling, unless we neutralize some of their strength through cultivating social intelligence, the common good, and social justice.

Social justice motivates us to act, especially when our interests are strengthened by families' histories of multigenerational involvement in social justice issues. Because we are all subjected to multigenerational influences from our families, whether we realize this or not, social justice helps us to assess the power of these influences in varied situations. For example, we use social intelligence to question the wisdom of multigenerational pressures. From our questioning, we may conclude that we must make our own decisions about assessing multigenerational realities and social justice, and that we must deliberately choose to dedicate time and energy to increasing social justice.

Social intelligence makes us more practical about the extent to which we allow ourselves to be guided by social justice and multigenerational realities. When we understand the impacts of our families on our social intelligence, we become more objective and critical about whether to succumb to powerful family influences, especially in relation to social justice interests.

Historical Actors

When we become aware of the power and complexities of families, beliefs, social classes, cultures, and societies we gain social intelligence, which guides us in how we understand and achieve social justice. Establishing social justice is a meaningful and purposeful goal, which attends to the needs and rights of all, as well as creates viable ways to improve social conditions in societies and history. The challenge of increasing our social intelligence, so that we can act as historical actors, brings fulfillment in the long run, and satisfies our existential needs to live as fully as possible.

Because our families are our most intense emotional systems, we need to first learn how to be responsible about defining ourselves in our relationships to intimate others, which includes being aware of who we are, as well as recognizing the emotional climates of our families. For example, we pay attention to the non-rational pressures that relatives use to ensure that we conform sufficiently to families' cultures and values. We reach these goals of understanding and action in our families when we establish missions based on social intelligence principles that identify broad pictures of our current situations.

Broad views of social realities make us more objective about ourselves and our opportunities to initiate individual and social changes. They encourage us to assess social justice in varied social settings as well as our families. However, we learn about ourselves and gain social intelligence, by deliberately creating foundations of our social intelligence in the midst of the emotional give-and-take of our families. The crucibles of our families test us for who we are, what we believe, and what we want to accomplish.

Being historical actors in our families requires that we meet family responsibilities, and at the same time accomplish constructive tasks in our communities and the world. This means that we continue to pay attention to life cycle needs among our relatives, as well as to economic needs for physical survival, education, and celebration. Family and community tasks change constantly, and are not easy to accomplish, but social intelligence guides us and helps us to be effective in following through with our most ambitious social justice goals. For example, even though we most likely cannot accomplish what we want, we must at least stand firm in pursuing what we care about the most.

Just as social intelligence helps us to recognize what social justice is, and the extent to which social justice exists, social intelligence also shows us the challenges and values of resolving social justice issues in our families. We take nothing for granted, even though we may not have answers to the many questions we must ask, such as: what are the assumptions we make about family members? To what extent do family expectations limit the choices of family members? How can we meet family needs in the fairest ways possible? How can we distinguish between relatives' real needs and imagined needs? How can we continue to define ourselves in relation to other family members?

These questions, and their answers, encourage habits of being objective in our personal relationships, so that we are neither exploited by nor drained of our vital life energies by generously trying to meet the unreal needs of others. We must learn how to cultivate mature ways to balance our social assessments, so that we use our social intelligence for productive purposes, and at the same time continue to grow by increasing our social intelligence. These viable strategies apply social intelligence in order to achieve social justice in our families and other social settings.

Being historical actors coordinates our efforts. We do not lose advantages as historical actors, because we maintain broad social intelligence perspectives on our lives, while simultaneously meeting personal needs. For example, we honor the power and complexities of the five major social influences of families, beliefs, social classes, cultures, and societies in whatever we do both within and outside our families. Consequently, we recognize that our families are the most essential and most intense social systems in which we develop and learn to establish constructive postures toward ourselves, others, and the world.

Family Responsibilities

Family responsibilities are not political issues, but universal concerns which need our attention if our families and societies are to thrive. Social intelligence does not articulate specific aspects of family responsibilities to be concerned about, but rather presents universal needs to be met for our family members, especially those who are the most dependent on others for their survival. We use social intelligence to increase our autonomy by understanding some of the difficulties that result from being caught up in the emotional dynamics of our families. This is important because people often tend to prolong their emotional dependencies, rather than free themselves and others to be socially intelligent historical actors or pioneers in social justice.

Historically, religions incorporated moral codes about many different family responsibilities in their beliefs and practices, so it is not too far a stretch of the imagination to consider that social justice—as well as religions—suggest a wide range of different ways to think about family standards and family issues. For example, those who work for social justice understand that family abuses are integral aspects of family interactions that must be noticed and avoided as much as possible. Similarly, social intelligence uses social facts about intense family emotional systems to deepen our understanding about gross aberrations in family behavior, so that we face problems of family violence by getting more in charge of some of the destructive aspects of families' reactivity.

Both social intelligence and social justice suggest that we must acknowledge the dark sides of our families, and that not all family members are able to meet their responsibilities for nurturing or protecting their young and needy family members. Family responsibilities are necessarily related to achieving family essentials, while at the same time striving to create conditions for the optimal development and accomplishment of all family members. However, it is often our ineptness at living up to our family responsibilities that makes us reexamine our social intelligence and social justice concerns. For example, we realize that social intelligence helps us to gain some control over our non-rational behavior, so that we are more realistic—rather than idealistic—in caring for our families.

Unless we use social intelligence to see the broader pictures of our families, family trends, and international family needs, we are likely to miss the social fact that doing our best to care for others is all that is required of us to be responsible. For example, being over-responsible for other family members may actually prove hazardous, because no one benefits from excesses of over-caring. Consequently, we need to be practical in meeting the real needs of others, so that both we and they are sufficiently free and independent to live fully. When we cater only to the imagined needs of family members—needs imagined by either them or us—we all too easily debilitate the recipients of our attentions, because imbalances in meeting family responsibilities do little more than perpetuate intense emotional dependencies.

One of the emphases of social intelligence is that we should aim to meet only real family responsibilities before we venture forth to increase the common good or social justice as socially intelligent human beings. Because neither social intelligence nor social justice denies or ignores basic family needs, family dependents are consistently high priorities among our family concerns. Nevertheless, dealing with family needs is not the only responsibility that family members have. After we have met family responsibilities reasonably well, we are ready to broaden our horizons to include possibilities for making community contributions or initiating social changes in societies. These ventures gradually increase our social intelligence, so that we are ultimately more effective in pursuing and achieving social justice goals.

Establishing these priorities is significant, because they allow us to make more consolidated efforts to organize our daily activities around value choices that bring about increased equality, inclusiveness, diversity, cooperation, and openness in our families and societies. For example, we do not allow ourselves to dwell on the dark side of family life, when we immerse ourselves and stay committed to projects which improve our social and emotional conditions. Rather, we are sufficiently free to think clearly, so that we work toward goals which create meaningful contributions to both local and global communities.

Conflicts and Losses

Because families are the most intense emotional systems to which we belong, we frequently experience our most severe conflicts in our families, as well as feel our deepest losses with respect to our relatives. We live in close proximity—emotionally rather than geographically—to our relatives, so that we tend to compete with them more strongly than with our friends or peers. Similarly, due to the fact that interdependence is long-lived in our families, we often feel our most acute pangs of loss when significant relatives die or leave our families for other reasons.

We use social intelligence both to resolve family conflicts and to deal with the loss of close relatives. For example, social intelligence helps us to see the broad pictures of our lives, so that we think more clearly about strategies and goals to achieve, which in turn enables us to deal effectively with conflicts and losses.

When we realize the futility of investing our energies in fighting with relatives, and at the same time understand that we can accomplish constructive goals with our resources, we are less likely to let conflicts absorb our energies for months or years. Consequently, we negotiate with others to achieve purposeful, meaningful, and productive goals. We also decide to grieve or mourn appropriately for lost relatives, so that we can then get on with our lives. Even when our family losses cut to the quick of our being, especially if they are unexpected, we can resolve to move on by making the world a better place.

By contrast, our momentums toward progress—which include cultivating social intelligence and social justice—are slowed down considerably if we do not maintain broad perspectives on us and our worlds while we suffer from conflicts and losses. If our conflicts and losses are chronic, for example, we may drift into slow declines rather than express our anxieties through reconciliation or grieving. However, when we know that we want to avoid developing dysfunctions in our families, we face up to our conflicts and losses, and resolve them by assuming tasks that help us to express or transcend our anger and grief.

These socially intelligent processes do not focus on describing and explaining unhealthy denials of conflicts and losses in our families, but rather outline optimal possibilities for coping with life's hardest blows. Furthermore, when we call upon social intelligence and social justice to increase purpose in our lives, these strategies fill the vacuums created by the conflicts and losses in our families. Social intelligence shows us that when we focus on whatever needs to be done next, rather than on extending unproductive family conflicts or wallowing in repetitive grief, we benefit ourselves and others.

Even though we may not have initiated many of the circumstances directly connected to conflicts and losses in our families—for example, we may inherit our family conflicts from other relatives, or inadvertently become victims of the unrecognized and untreated symptoms of relatives' illnesses—we are responsible for our own reactions to ongoing conflicts and unexpected deaths. When we have young children, it is particularly important to be vigilant about how we deal with the conflicts and losses that come our way without looking for them. Our thoughtful, socially intelligent actions help us to take charge of our destinies at these times, if only in order to avoid becoming victims of circumstance.

Social intelligence continues to fortify our purposeful adaptations to conflicts and losses, while at the same time social justice supplies us with replacement goals for conflicts and losses. For example, we survive conflicts and losses most constructively and effectively when we use our everyday experiences to strengthen our capacities for social intelligence or our commitments to social justice. Meaningful, purposeful actions keep us moving toward bettering ourselves and our societies. Otherwise, we run the risk of continuing to be conflicted or bereft, because we are unable to meet our own survival needs to recover from severe emotional tensions and anxieties. Social intelligence guides us toward increasing social justice, so that we and others eventually benefit from the intense pain of our family conflicts and losses.

Fulfillment

In many respects people look to their families for fulfillment. For example, we see families as sources of intimacy; the good life of loving and being loved; the deep satisfaction of living meaningfully through interacting with relatives who share similar values; as well as sources of practical knowledge about how to play traditional roles such as being an adult child, spouse, parent, and grandparent. However, our dreams of fulfillment are more easily said than done, especially in modern times when family traditions are called into question, as well as the importance of families in our early and adult years. Consequently, families and family responsibilities are often avoided rather than accorded the reverence and awe that is still their due, given the power and complexities of families' emotional systems.

Because we often learn about values and morals in our families—including what not to do as well as what to do—we develop particular orientations toward ourselves and the world from our early beginnings as curious children. Nevertheless, when we are adults we have endless opportunities to remake our value choices if we so desire, making it possible for us to neutralize or disregard particular values and beliefs which are not productive in our lives. Furthermore, if we consider that our families have treated some of our relatives unjustly, we may choose to set things right by trying to change imbalances in our families' most emotion-laden bonds.

When our dreams of family fulfillment contrast starkly with family realities, we can usefully prepare ourselves to be on the ready to make adjustments in how we relate to our family members. As a result, our constructive responses make us more mature, socially intelligent, responsible adults, who strive to create more just social conditions in our families, especially for those in the youngest generations. We can also assess and act productively, on social facts about the extent to which our families treat their members with equal attention, so that all relatives thrive and do well in interacting with others in the world at large. Although this is a daunting agenda that cannot be accomplished easily or perfectly, it is also a meaningful direction to take, because it is in the interests of like-minded relatives as well as ourselves.

Social intelligence helps us to address these issues in others' families as well as our own. Being active members of families is a hassle as well as a privilege, but we all benefit from increasing our commitments to improve qualities of our family interactions. For example, at the same time that social intelligence fortifies us to make bold changes in how our families operate, we look toward social justice to help us to claim sufficient freedom to be effective historical actors in broad social arenas.

Whenever we choose to survive by sustaining the benefits of our intergenerational family emotional systems, we can use our families' patterns of behavior as ways to modify unwelcome impacts of the four other major social influences of beliefs, social classes, cultures, and societies. Social intelligence teaches us that families are foundations and sources that establish who we are and what we do, and also that when we understand our families, we are more astute in recognizing the particular power and complexities of beliefs, social classes, cultures, and societies. All in all social intelligence prepares us to be responsible historical actors, especially when we relate social intelligence principles to the moral ideals of social justice.

Even though we may not think that these different aspects of our journeys to live fully are fulfilling in themselves, in retrospect we can re-assess our starting points and see some of the gains we have made from being more socially intelligent and more aware of social justice in the conduct of our everyday lives. Knowing that we have an existential imperative to live fully—which includes enjoying the many different riches of modern industrial societies—helps us to persist in making decisions and commitments based on social intelligence and social justice. Our fulfillment and objectives predictably improve when we decide to make new value choices in the present for the future.

III. Beliefs and Social Justice

Beliefs are the second of the five basic dimensions of social intelligence—families, beliefs, social classes, cultures, and societies—which have strong impacts on how we think about social justice and the goals we choose to pursue in order to accomplish social justice. In some respects, however, it is easier to associate beliefs with social justice than families, because we usually consider family emotional processes to be private and personal rather than public. Furthermore, we do not connect the intensity of our family experiences with social justice as readily as we find affinities between our beliefs and social justice.

In spite of these relationships between families, beliefs, and social justice, social intelligence requires us to acknowledge that many of our beliefs derive from our families. For example, we learn how to understand ourselves, others, communities, societies, and globalization through our families, particularly according to the perspectives of the most dominant members of our families. Also, because we learn many of our beliefs from our relatives, we need to acknowledge that our beliefs can be changed, especially by interacting with our families in new ways, once we realize what the specific family sources are of our most deep-seated beliefs.

In addition, our families deliberately expose us to other significant sources of beliefs when we are children, and during the many years we need to grow into mature adults. For example, our religious and secular educations are laden with beliefs which are frequently rooted in our local communities. For example, during early stages of our development, we tend to be strongly influenced by leaders outside our families—in places of worship or schools—so that we tend to absorb some of their beliefs, partly due to the leaders' social status and hierarchical authority in the eyes of our parents and local communities.

Community beliefs, as well as family beliefs, are often difficult to change because they form the original essence of who we think we are and what we choose to do with our lives. Also, however much we assume that we have grown out of these deep-seated beliefs, the fact that we once held them means that they haunt us involuntarily from time to time throughout our adult years. For example, strong sentiments of joy or loss frequently evoke beliefs that have long outlived their usefulness for us.

Our beliefs in right and wrong, as well as our beliefs in social justice, are formed by our most significant experiences during early stages of our development. Therefore, because questioning is such a vital part of social intelligence and understanding social justice, we inevitably realize the values and complexities of social justice fully only in mature adulthood. Just as it takes time for us to grow, by increasing our social intelligence through our everyday routines, we cannot immediately usefully apply many of the ideals and abstractions of social justice issues in our exchanges with others.

One way we sharpen our appreciation of the meanings of social justice is to use social intelligence to scrutinize our beliefs, so that we become more aware of which beliefs help us to deepen our understanding of self and others, and which beliefs are productive or unproductive for our socially intelligent purposes of acting to increase the common good. Although the common good and social justice are not synonymous, becoming more socially intelligent, through increasing the common good, prepares us to make the commitments necessary to work with others to accomplish social justice. For example, the common good may be adequately realized by accomplishing fairly narrow local goals, rather than by changing value choices now to build more socially just societies in the present for the future.

However, in the long run beliefs are significant aspects of our socially intelligent trajectories to accomplish both the common good and social justice, because they motivate us and bring meaning, purpose, and enthusiasm to our missions of accomplishing constructive goals. When we learn sufficient social facts about problems in our societies, we become more responsible historical actors, who persist in working to improve social conditions for all through diverse quests to increase social justice. Critical aspects of beliefs and social justice are described and explained in this chapter of *Social Intelligence and Social Justice*, in order to make it easier to come to terms with these major social influences in both local and global settings.

Emotional Systems

Whereas families are sometimes defined as emotional systems, due to family members' interdependence and patterns of interaction, we more accurately think of beliefs as subtle but powerful mechanisms that bind like-minded people together. For example, both families and social groups unite around their shared beliefs to some extent, and the emotional content of these shared beliefs—as well as how intensely our beliefs are held—create the harmony or unity of those who share beliefs.

Religious, political, and secular beliefs rooted in sciences, arts, and particular skills such as sports, are examples of how beliefs may galvanize individuals, groups, communities, and sometimes whole societies. Depending on the intensity and durability of our beliefs, their substantive meanings become particularly important predispositions in attitudes and motives for accomplishing specific tasks. For example, we may be defined as Christian or Muslim because of our beliefs, and consequently we tend to act in specific ways as Christians or Muslims. Similarly, our political beliefs may define our attitudes, opportunities, and life outcomes, often depending on the intensity of our beliefs. Therefore, social intelligence teaches us to be vigilant in cultivating our beliefs, because their emotional content may propel us in positive or negative directions throughout our lives.

Assuming that most adults use several different ways to define themselves through their beliefs, we need to assess whether our beliefs are helpful or limiting with respect to achieving our life goals. How do our beliefs serve us well or otherwise? To what extent does social intelligence show us that particular social facts reinforce or challenge our basic beliefs? Are we proceeding in ways which bring fruition to our deepest beliefs? Or, would we be better served by finding beliefs which allow us to explore new directions in whatever we do on a daily basis?

When we take social intelligence seriously and apply it to our beliefs and behavior, we become more critical of how productively or unproductively we spend our emotional energies. Emotions are not a disadvantage, but rather sources of powerful energies which we can choose to use in particular ventures. Therefore, it is consistently to our advantage that we realize where our emotional energies are spent, because then we can more easily make adjustments in our beliefs, so that we express our most deep-seated emotions through our actions.

For example, we may yearn to enter the healing professions and yet dislike the scientific content of available study programs that would allow us to pursue these goals. When we use social intelligence to see the broader pictures of our lives, however, we can deliberately increase our curiosity about health sciences and health studies, by following our deep interests to discover health-related knowledge that truly fascinates us. Ideally, our new explorations are guided by our social intelligence, as well as our awareness of the emotional content of our beliefs, so that we can gradually discard any negative emotions we have about science, such as fears, in order to pursue genuine interests in science and health.

Social intelligence encourages us to increase our awareness about the importance of all our most emotional beliefs, by checking our beliefs with social facts. For example, we benefit from examining our political and artistic beliefs in terms of their emotional and factual content, in order to ensure that we are not wasting our valuable emotional investments on pursuing impossible goals for the future.

Editing the emotional content of our current beliefs helps us to clear the way for examining beliefs in social justice more effectively. Such scrutiny helps us to be more productive in whatever we undertake, so that we choose more freely whether or not we want to get more deeply involved in particular social justice concerns. Consequently, our beliefs in social justice grow and become more powerful motives in our everyday lives.

The broad perspectives of social intelligence continue to guide us in assessing the five major social influences of families, beliefs, social classes, cultures, and societies, as well as sharpen our understanding of weak links in our chains of being and acting. When we are more objective in recognizing the toll that emotional investments in nonproductive beliefs take in our lives, we more readily make new value choices to increase social intelligence, the common good, and social justice. Becoming more emotionally invested in social justice gradually encourages actions and accomplishments that serve us and others more effectively.

Historical Sources

Our beliefs do not become significant parts of our lives because they operate in a vacuum, but rather our beliefs have strong influences on our behavior due to their social and cultural connections. Similarly, it is not only because of the social and cultural sources of our beliefs today that they have power over our decisions, but because our beliefs have histories of their own, which are directly related to our personal life experiences. Thus we are products of overlapping histories in complex ways, and understanding the historical sources of our beliefs helps us to be more objective and critical about their influences, especially with regard to our interests in social justice.

We must first assess how we nurtured our beliefs in who we are and how we conduct ourselves in our everyday lives. Consequently, we benefit from understanding how our beliefs influence what we want to accomplish in our lifetimes. Because being socially intelligent requires that we use our beliefs productively—we need to recognize which beliefs support us in our most cherished goals, and which beliefs detract from our aspirations to contribute to the common good and social justice.

Just as we understand who we are and what we want to accomplish through our most longstanding beliefs, we also need to examine how we understand the common good and social justice through our beliefs. For example, which of our parents first aroused our interests in sustaining empathy or altruism in how we view ourselves and others? To what extent were our relatives aware or unaware of social justice? To what extent do we experience our families as fair or just?

In order to examine these themes responsibly, we increase our social intelligence by using each of the five dimensions of social intelligence to see and assess historical sources of our beliefs. Understanding the power of historical sources of our beliefs derives from looking closely at who we are and what we want to accomplish in relation to our families, social classes, cultures, and societies. Our historical reflections strengthen our capacities to be objective in understanding and using our beliefs to achieve social justice goals.

Family histories show us how we absorbed relatives' beliefs in our most formative years. For example, when we look at intricate patterns in family communications or family support, we see how our positions in these exchanges influenced the messages we received from our relatives, their expectations, and the goals we aimed for as adults. Now that we examine and question the power of these social influences, we make it possible to change some of the patterns in multigenerational repetitions of behavior, attitudes, and motives in our families.

Our families' social class beliefs are other significant determining influences in how families interact, and how individual family members are launched into the world. When we use social intelligence to question our beliefs, we neutralize some of our relatives' power over how we conduct ourselves in everyday situations. Similarly, social class influences in our communities and societies determine who we think we are as well as what we want to accomplish. However, social intelligence also loosens the hold of social class expectations outside our families, because we see that other beliefs are more effective in achieving our goals and social justice.

Our quests to understand the historical sources of beliefs link us to many cultural and societal beliefs beyond our families. For example, social intelligence helps us to recognize that cultures support beliefs as part of the status quo of societies, as well as complex dimensions of personal and political freedom. Furthermore, we benefit from examining differences in religious beliefs which support or resist social changes and social justice, particularly by paying attention to beliefs in materialism, capitalism, and consumerism.

History itself is a significant social source of beliefs. Wars and political tensions influence patriotism, for example, so we can use social intelligence to identify ethnocentrism and national biases in our beliefs. Being more objective as we increase our social intelligence often loosens these questionable emotional ties. However, we need to continue to cultivate historical awareness of broad social influences in beliefs, if we are to understand histories of social justice and social issues.

Seeing personal life histories, in relation to histories of social justice, inspires us to narrow gaps between social justice ideals and social realities, especially in terms of social injustices in particular situations. We use history to see how the content and outreach of social justice beliefs change over time. For example, today we are more concerned about gender and sexual orientation rights, as well as standards of living in both under-developed and developed countries. Therefore, because globalization transforms our beliefs and social conditions, we benefit from strengthening beliefs in specific social justice values such as equality, inclusiveness, diversity, cooperation, and openness.

Historical Actors

Believing that we are historical actors often motivates us to be more socially intelligent and more socially responsible in whatever we decide to do with our lives. However, an important social fact is that each person is an historical actor, whether we are aware of this individual and social reality or not. Furthermore, we can surmise that people who believe that they are historical actors tend to make real differences in how things happen in the world.

When we become sufficiently aware of these social realities and possibilities about being historical actors, we often establish different priorities and pursue more altruistic goals. For example, if we are historical actors who believe that we have a particular purpose or mission to create opportunities for people who are less privileged than we are, we heighten our probabilities of accomplishing these goals. Being an effective historical actor largely depends on the qualities of our beliefs about being historical actors, as well as on identifying with other historical actors' priorities.

Understanding emotional systems of beliefs and historical sources of beliefs advances our awareness of ourselves as socially intelligent historical actors. For instance, we develop habits of thought that help us to assess the emotional content of specific beliefs as well as their historical and social sources, in order to be more objective in creating and choosing which beliefs to nurture as aware historical actors. We also need to choose strategies to manage our beliefs, by honoring beliefs that support our socially intelligent goals to increase the common good and social justice. Ultimately, increasing our socially intelligent beliefs helps us to be both practical and effective in accomplishing social justice goals.

Historical actors try to find ways to use emotions and emotional strategies to increase the common good and social justice. They also take care not to succumb to the lure of seeking emotional satisfactions when they need to make tough decisions. Social intelligence clears our minds, so that we make more accurate assessments of our social situations. This prepares us to accomplish goals that increase social justice in the long run; keeping our professional actions passionate fires our work with intensity, so that we stay motivated to increase social justice in spite of others' criticism or resistance. Choosing to express constructive emotions both preserves our integrity, and helps us to cope with supremely difficult, discouraging endeavors.

These skills are important for historical actors to develop. Being productive in making history increases our altruistic concerns, so that we choose to work with those who share our beliefs, in order to reach our goals more effectively. Using emotions fuels our efforts and maintains enthusiasm for our historical goals. Consequently, practical socially intelligent means help us to accomplish our goals, especially when they are grounded in historical facts.

Historical actors need social intelligence to leaven their understanding of social realities, and to discern opportunities that increase the common good and social justice. Social intelligence fortifies people's good intentions, so that new kinds of value choices are not only possible but wise. Historical actors who use social intelligence are less likely to get lost in the heady heights of aspiring to make historical moves to improve societies and civilizations. Although we need to aim high in formulating social justice goals, historical actors also keep their feet firmly on the ground, in order to recognize and deal with the new territories ahead.

Socially intelligent know-how enables us to be selective about choosing and investing emotions in our best purposes as historical actors. For example, we break down our next tasks into manageable segments, so that we can accomplish them together with those who follow our leads as historical actors. We stay involved with the past so that we do not repeat mistakes already made, but we also advance with eyes on both the present and the future, in order to construct the best possible future world. As socially intelligent historical actors, we act in relation to families, beliefs, social classes, cultures, and societies, so that we maintain some degree of control over creating the preferred social conditions we imagined as responsible historical actors.

Responsibilities

We are more likely to cultivate and refine our beliefs in responsibility when we consider our own responsibilities and want to be responsible. Social intelligence often helps us to arrive at this starting point of increased interest in responsibility, because we must have some awareness about human nature, as well as the power and complexities of societies, before we are sufficiently mature to decide what responsibility is and how we want to express it. It is also largely our own senses of responsibility that ultimately lead us to gain personal satisfaction and fulfillment. For example, when we think we are or have been responsible, we are usually pleased with what we accomplished.

Thus, in many respects social intelligence helps us to realize the importance of meeting our responsibilities in order to live fully and be fulfilled. However, our choices of socially intelligent goals need to be authentic in order for us to be responsible—social intelligence guides us to aspire to accomplish our preferred goals in contributing to our communities and societies. In addition, meeting our family responsibilities is a foundation for being socially intelligent and living fully, so this aspect of responsibility cannot be ignored in our assessments of who we are and what we want to accomplish in broad social spheres.

When we increase our understanding of how our families interact as emotional systems, we become more aware of who our family leaders and followers are, and the extent to which dominance and coercion are distinctive patterns in our family exchanges. Our socially intelligent know-how—which includes privileging social justice values such as equality, cooperation, and openness—shows us that being over-responsible in our families may make some family relationships unstable or dysfunctional. For example, adolescents often rebel against their parents' preferences, or their parents' overprotection which stifled the children's development. It is easy for children and adolescents to be too protected or too coddled to understand the ways of the world. Social intelligence shows us that we must maintain freedom and autonomy in our families if all relatives are to be mature and independent.

Questions about what responsibility is, and how much responsibility we should assume, need to be pondered and explored as we conduct our everyday lives. Because we learn by doing, only we can assess the extent to which we and others can afford behaviors that increase family dependence rather than independence. We do this by understanding broad dimensions of social responsibilities, as well as intimate aspects of personal responsibilities: what is the nature of romantic love and family care? Social intelligence encourages us to explore and examine a wide variety of responsibilities we could assume in our families, beliefs, social classes, cultures, and societies. Similarly, social justice helps us to assess the extent to which our contributions to the common good in our communities and societies reflect or pioneer social justice.

Our considerations of the nature of human nature, in making these socially intelligent assessments, need to be grounded in social facts. This is so because our tasks in being responsible historical actors include responding to real human needs rather than imagined needs. We are more objective in defining the real needs of individuals and groups when we consider which social facts are being expressed in the five major social influences of families, beliefs, social classes, cultures, and societies. What social realities of social class differences define opportunities and life outcomes? How do beliefs support or reduce our capacities to be responsible in accomplishing social justice goals? How can we learn to be effective through cooperative efforts to increase social intelligence and the common good?

Social intelligence emphasizes the importance of family and social emotional systems. A related social fact is that many of us are easily prevented from fulfilling our goals or missions by allowing non-rational beliefs to divert our attention away from them, thus decreasing our senses of responsibility. Consequently, in an historic age when having fun is considered to be a cultural ideal that cuts across all social classes, we often have little time and energy left to invest in worthwhile projects to improve the quality of life for all.

However, given these social realities, social intelligence suggests that our omnipresent tendencies to respond to emotional distractions should not be thought of as irreversible human traits. Rather, social intelligence strengthens our hope that we can learn how to restore responsibility to its honored place in our beliefs, which ultimately makes us more effective in improving social conditions for all.

Conflicts and Losses

We need to recognize not only the power and complexities of the five major social influences of families, beliefs, social classes, cultures, and societies in determining life conditions for populations, but also the ways in which these social influences direct individuals' and groups' emotional reactions and emotional investments. For example, we benefit from examining particular conflicts and losses that are integral parts of our social conditions and established ways of doing things.

As in our families, conflicts and losses in our communities and societies can wreak havoc on our best efforts to keep the peace or take care of necessary tasks. Even though social intelligence does not spell out many clear-cut characteristics of the nature of human nature, beyond basic significant dimensions such as the dominance of social and emotional qualities in our associations and interactions, we can understand that we often enter into conflicts with others too quickly, as well as react negatively to involuntary losses which limit our material or emotional resources. For example, much of our personal life is easily caught up in dealing with family conflicts or job opportunity losses.

We often allow conflicts and losses to hold us back from achieving our most cherished social justice goals. Because we commit our emotions to support ideals of family love or professional success, we are easily drained when things do not go well. Consequently, our visions of better futures are dimmed, and our enthusiasm for increasing social intelligence and social justice wanes. However, social intelligence signals that we need to call a halt to these effects of conflicts and losses, by watching and changing our emotional investments in particular projects. Making deliberate shifts in our emotional investments reduces our vulnerability to crises in conflicts and losses.

We examine conflicts and losses in our beliefs, as well as in our families, social classes, cultures, and societies, in order to use social intelligence to loosen the grip of crises in conflicts and losses, especially when we most need to advance toward social justice goals. Because social intelligence anchors our social justice aims, we learn how to stabilize our unique or recurring concerns about conflicts and losses. For example, we highlight our concerns about conflicts and losses in our beliefs, so that we gradually decrease our involvement in them and increase our social intelligence.

One sign that our beliefs are not sufficiently strong to take us toward better future societies is the number of conflicts we nurture among our beliefs. For example, do we talk about the importance of education for improving the world, but at the same time refuse to investigate study programs seriously? Are we shocked by global poverty while we simultaneously ignore the poverty that exists in our own cities? Do we choose careers that reward us financially, without paying attention to the broad social needs that affect us all? These are significant questions to ask in determining the extent to which we are true to our deepest beliefs, or ready to make contributions to the common good and social justice, rather than doggedly following our most remunerative options.

Social intelligence encourages us to adjust our beliefs in many different ways. For example, we try to understand existing conflicts in our beliefs more fully, because these drain our energies, and prevent us from increasing the common good and social justice. Not only do we identify conflicts in our beliefs, but we also set ourselves the tasks of discovering the social sources of our conflicting beliefs. Where do our conflicting beliefs come from? Whom did we try to emulate in developing and articulating these conflicting beliefs? How can we change beliefs which hold us back from accomplishing our most cherished goals?

Conflicts in beliefs are not solely manifested in personal contexts. They often reflect conflicts between different social classes, ethnicities, genders, sexual orientations, religions, educations, political affiliations, or ambitions. We are integral parts of broad social systems, as well as family emotional systems, and we may choose to eradicate—or at least minimize—some aspects of public social conflicts in our beliefs, as well as conflicts in our personal beliefs. For example, we may opt to work with others to narrow social class extremes in wealth and education, so that we decrease the frequency of conflicts in current or future communities and societies.

Our beliefs in losses impact us in broad ways as well as personally. For example, we frequently mourn our spent childhoods, because they were not perfect. Consequently, we may be engulfed by powerlessness because we feel we lost so many opportunities that we cannot create better futures now. Or, we may think that our genders limit our options, and that we are restricted to particular career paths. Sometimes, we experience limited options as losses of privileges, rather than pay attention to what we can do now, in spite of our beliefs in past losses due to stereotypes, prejudices, and discrimination.

Social intelligence encourages us to see how important our many different beliefs in losses are in determining our decisions and commitments. Losses, decisions, and commitments have strong emotional components, and these emotional investments need to be constructive if we are to achieve social justice as historical actors. When we are motivated to grow from the deepest losses that we and our communities have experienced, we can usually use socially intelligent perspectives more fully to inspire our beliefs, rather than stay captive to negative beliefs in losses.

We resolve conflicts and losses in our beliefs by acknowledging both personal and broad social aspects of our conflicts and losses. Although this assessment may be a difficult drawn-out process, we begin to move in more constructive directions when we let social intelligence guide us. We take stock of our conflicts and losses, so that our emotions are sufficiently free to support and speed us in creating improved, socially just societies.

Fulfillment

In some important respects we cannot be fulfilled unless we believe that fulfillment is possible for ourselves and others. We may make our lives more meaningful—especially by increasing our social intelligence, the common good, or social justice—but unless we deliberately cultivate values which reinforce experiences of fulfillment, our beliefs may fall short in supporting this benefit or goal. When we consider beliefs and social justice in this chapter of *Social Intelligence and Social Justice*, we pay attention to the fact that actually achieving fulfillment necessarily depends on our beliefs in fulfillment, and what fulfillment means to each one of us.

This approach to understanding fulfillment does not invite the idea that we live in isolation from others and can dream up exactly what we want to do, but rather that we need to explore families, social classes, cultures, and societies in order to understand how we developed our beliefs in fulfillment, and how we can go about changing these beliefs when we identify contradictions or inadequacies in them. For example, socially intelligent approaches to changing our beliefs in individual and social fulfillment help us take deliberate measures to bring them more under our control.

In the long run, our actions define our beliefs in some of the same ways that our beliefs predispose us to certain experiences. Even though we may not particularly believe that fulfillment is possible, we can take actions that presuppose fulfillment is possible. For example, we learn to trust and let go of our growing children because we want them to be fulfilled. Consequently, we find that when we act as though our children's fulfillment is possible, we increase our own fulfillment as well as the fulfillment of others. Acting in this way expresses our belief that good parenting ultimately includes relinquishing control over our children, so that adult freedoms are shared, enjoyed, and fulfilled productively.

Social intelligence requires us to maintain objectivity by continuing to pay attention to social facts. For example, we assess the results of our decisions and commitments by checking them with social facts, rather than by merely accepting that trying to meet our goals brings fulfillment. When we are socially intelligent, we need to do whatever we possibly can to actually meet our goals before we indulge ourselves in feelings of fulfillment. Fulfillment is therefore an earned consequence of striving to use socially intelligent means—including working with others—to do whatever we set out to do. We check the social facts of our achievements against our aspirations, so that our beliefs in fulfillment are not based on false hopes or delusions of success. Furthermore, although seeking the truth about our progress toward social justice may be discouraging, we learn to appreciate incremental changes in our situations, and in our capacities to be socially intelligent.

Even though our collective work toward achieving social justice cannot be finished in our lifetimes, we can cut down the tasks we undertake according to the nature of the problems tackled, or the time involved in sustaining our shared efforts. For example, we decide to work with others toward passing legislation that allows less privileged children to have access to computers, rather than aim to transform a national system of education. Having a narrow but realistic goal reflects the spirit of social intelligence, and at the same time we learn how not to give up our overall social justice efforts to level inequalities in education in the long run.

Similarly, we cut down the size of our tasks to increase social justice by reducing the time-frames of our assessments of success to day-by-day or hour-by-hour efforts. Thus, we gain fulfillment by focusing on what we think we should be doing to achieve social justice now. For example, if we believe that we have been successful on a particular day, we feel fulfilled because we know that we are doing whatever we can to improve our shared futures now. We do not deceive ourselves about the complexity of the social justice tasks in hand, or our achievements. Rather, we see that we have made some impacts on tenacious social justice issues, and we believe that these support our continued commitments to social justice and better futures.

IV. Social Classes and Social Justice

Social classes are the third major dimension of social intelligence that influences how we think and act in relation to social justice. Together with families, beliefs, cultures, and societies, social classes describe and explain ways in which individuals and populations tend to get caught up easily with strong social influences that affect significant aspects of their lives, however much they may prefer to be free and independent. By contrast, social intelligence is an effective means to increase control over these powerful social class influences. Social intelligence also encourages individuals, groups, and societies to improve our present and future worlds, so that by creating alternatives to social classes, we increase social justice and cooperation rather than competition and conflict.

Social classes are powerful and complex social influences in their own right. Until now most societies, in all times and all places, have organized their members in social hierarchies, which define statuses as well as ways to relate to each other. Even though we may believe that the power of history and social traditions is sufficient reason to perpetuate existing social classes, we inevitably benefit from considering alternative ways to organize ourselves—such as by honoring more balanced and more equal relationships with others—so that all members of our populations gain more meaningful shares of our combined resources.

Our existing social classes limit different people's access to societies' privileges and honors. Even though these exclusions are generally understood to be justified to some extent, we cannot afford to live in societies that do not meet the basic needs of all. Social intelligence helps us to develop strategies and practical solutions to these social issues, while at the same time social justice motivates us to pursue ideals and values that create more viable living conditions for whole populations in the present and future. Although these goals may seem abstract, there is nothing more practical than to seek the rectification of some of the most destructive social consequences from having inadequate distributions of resources. For example, we cannot achieve satisfactory levels of education for all members of our populations, until we devise more widespread distributions of adequate resources and opportunities.

When we see some of the emotional systems components of our existing social classes—for example, the many different ways we feel pressured to conform to the social class dictates of more powerful social classes—we gain a clearer view and firmer grasp of the options we need in order to free ourselves. We also gain from reviewing some of the most significant social facts about social classes through history to some extent, so that we can live up to the diverse challenges of being historical actors in the present for the future. Thus, social intelligence heightens our awareness of social realities in the world around us, which helps us to anchor social justice ideals in actions that bring about better worlds.

In due course, social intelligence also clarifies our responsibilities as historical actors, so that we find and collaborate with like-minded others to increase the common good and social justice. For example, recognizing social class influences in our behavior sheds light on how to act in the most creative, constructive ways possible. Consequently, we do not shirk from our responsibilities to provide for all, while simultaneously assessing our conflicts and losses, but rather proceed more effectively toward fulfillment.

In these respects, social intelligence helps us to keep on track with our missions to create better worlds for present and future generations. The alertness we gain from being socially intelligent is not superficial, but rather deepens our commitments to reliable, imaginative knowledge and social justice. For example, when we are discouraged or weary, we can choose to turn to social justice to inspire our actions, so that we live in closer accord with relatively new values such as equality, inclusiveness, diversity, cooperation, and openness, which increase our senses of purpose and fulfillment. Consequently, we are neither complacent nor fatalistic. Rather, we are ready and well-prepared to be tested, with regard to our beliefs and capacities to be socially intelligent, in whatever we undertake to change social classes for the common good and social justice.

Emotional Systems

Social classes may be thought of as open-ended emotional systems, because people in different social classes react to each other both positively and negatively in some of the same ways as families and communities who have shared or opposing beliefs. For example, social classes are emotional systems that range from being orderly or controlled to disorderly or essentially out of control. Whether or not social classes are viable often depends on the maturity of their members, as well as their senses of responsibility for each other and people who are outside their classes. Optimal social classes have flexible relationship systems that adapt effectively to each other rather than repeat unproductive historical conflicts.

Although the social realities of social classes are often far from harmonious, social classes have different levels of emotional intensity. For example, different social classes are emotional systems to some extent, because their members frequently experience social classes as either limiting their options, or as being supportive for making innovative contributions to others. Consequently, we need to ask ourselves—especially in relation to social justice concerns—whether or not our social classes truly work for us in society by providing opportunities to make constructive contributions to all.

Social intelligence helps us to adapt to the social realities of our social classes, so that to some extent we appreciate social classes' stamina and power in defining our views of ourselves, the world, and our actions. For example, we are independent or dependent largely because of the emotional impacts of specific patterns of interactions, such as those found in both our families and our social classes. Furthermore, although we can choose to change our interactions when we understand the restrictiveness of some of our social class dependencies, it is often difficult to do so, and may be impossible to accomplish until we are more aware of our own participation in problematic dependencies with our families and our social classes.

Our awareness of social classes as emotional social systems helps us to be more objective and critical about who we are and what we want to accomplish. This objectivity enables us to see how people are not treated equally, for example, and how we can increase social justice as individuals, families, and societies. Recognizing social and emotional realities in our social classes enables us to move in practical directions, which makes the attainment of social ideals like social justice more possible.

Social intelligence clarifies our thinking about social issues in social classes, as well as social concerns in our families and beliefs, so that we take more enlightened actions to deliberately create egalitarian social conditions for social justice. At the same time that we reduce the impacts of social barriers that prevent us from achieving our preferred goals, for example, we find that we invest more energy in constructive goals to increase the common good and social justice. Moreover, considering our social classes as emotional systems on a daily basis helps us to recognize and understand other emotional systems in societies—such as our cultures—that also sometimes prevent us from achieving what we really want to accomplish.

When we use social intelligence to acknowledge emotional systems in our social classes and other social settings, we sharpen our awareness of the many subtle ways in which we accommodate to others in defining our daily routines and major goals. For example, when we make living up to others' expectations a high priority, we avoid taking risks to improve the quality of life for all members of our populations. Therefore, if we try only to meet others' expectations, we shirk our true responsibilities to achieve social justice.

Although we may not readily understand how social classes are connected to achieving social justice, we can usually see that increasing our social intelligence prepares us to stand up to others in order to do what we need to do. Consequently, we must not merely stay well-intentioned about how to increase social justice, but rather be ever-ready to take advantage of opportunities that increase the common good for all through our actions. Only when we consider everyone's rights to live fully can we see beyond the short-range immediacies of our demanding, pressing social class emotional systems. Thus, our knowledge of social classes as emotional systems helps us to accomplish practical goals for individuals and societies in the present for the future.

Historical Sources

Families' emotional systems connect family members in several generations to each other, so that family members often experience strong relationship bonds in spite of not actually knowing their relatives or ancestors. Multigenerational sources of information—which include past generations' social class affiliations—reach back in time beyond our modern conventional families of parents and children, and at the same time impact our present social class memberships. For example, to the extent that our families lived through histories of deprived social class conditions, we may tend to carry on some of the same patterns of interdependence, forged by our ancestors, that were crucial for their survival.

Even though social intelligence shows us that multigenerational realities from the past can be changed in the present for the future to some extent, it is often difficult to identify and modify the rootedness of our past and present emotional dependencies. Past patterns of family interaction reveal social class actions, goals, and orientations in our families that impact our understanding of the importance of social class loyalties in our present social relationships and attitudes.

Persistent family and social class links in our personal histories connect us to local, national, and global histories. We personalize the impacts of history on who we are, and how we are connected to social classes, through examining family experiences and community bonds, as well as the broad historical contexts of societies and international communities. For example, if our countries are at war we not only suffer from changes in our family routines, but also from dramatic shifts in national events due to the impacts of personal and historical losses.

To the extent that our family histories shed light on the many ways in which history shapes our social class experiences, we become aware of the significance of social classes in our lives today for the future. For example, history connects us to the injustices of the past and present, and motivates us to make constructive contributions to the common good now, in order to improve our societies in the future. We not only recognize the repetitiveness of social class tensions through different generations, but also seriously consider possibilities for changing existing social classes. In these respects, social intelligence guides us to create pragmatic strategies to reduce some of the destructive consequences of social classes for all members of our populations.

Social intelligence teaches us about the tenacious restrictiveness of past and present social classes, so that we work toward increasing opportunities between social classes more effectively. For example, we may choose to assign ourselves—and those with whom we work—particular tasks which reduce some of the extreme contrasts in having access to available resources between the members of upper and lower social classes. This historical mission develops only when we realize the power and complexities of the social classes in which we participate. Consequently, we become more pragmatic in reducing and even eliminating some destructive social class influences in our own lives and the lives of others.

History is our guide for understanding social classes, and for assessing the successes and failures of social classes in the past and present. Examining social facts related to social class deprivations and social injustices in the past motivates us to persist in our efforts to build better worlds today for tomorrow. Our social justice ideals guide our socially intelligent actions, so that we see more clearly how the different aspects of social intelligence—families, beliefs, social classes, cultures, and societies—influence social conditions of social justice— such as equality, inclusiveness, diversity, cooperation, and openness.

Objectivity about social facts in social injustices increases our social intelligence. This allows us to focus more attentively on concerns about social classes in personal, national, and global histories. Social intelligence sheds light on how social class conditions in our individual lives are linked through the major social influences of families, beliefs, social classes, cultures, and societies to the attainment of our preferred social class goals for improved futures. Consequently, our reliance on historical sources enables us to create more constructive histories now, so that we build futures that are not merely predetermined by our flawed social classes.

Historical Actors

Social intelligence anchors our efforts to achieve social justice by reducing the restrictive impacts of social classes. For example, when we see social inequalities in social classes, we often become uneasy about the continued widening differences between upper and lower classes in societies, as well as the growing contrasts between upper and lower global social classes. However, because hierarchies of social classes persist in all societies and the global community, we can use social intelligence to learn how to identify contrasts in opportunities more clearly, and to do something constructive about them.

Social intelligence anchors our strategies to bring about reforms in social class structures, as well as more universal access to resources, because we develop social intelligence from observing and reporting social facts. Also, when we are aware of the substance of significant social issues about social classes, that impact the lives of all members of our populations, we are more likely to find like-minded others who will work with us to achieve goals that remedy current social class ills.

Ideally we are aware historical actors who take on tasks aimed at increasing social justice in social classes. Because social classes are complex and powerful, we must create as solid foundations of social intelligence as possible, which are achieved through examining interactions in families, beliefs, social classes, cultures, and societies. For example, we benefit from understanding how the emotional investments that people make in their families, beliefs, social classes, cultures, and societies either block communications and privileges, or open up communications and access to resources so that more people thrive.

Even though it is accurate to say that everyone is an historical actor by merely being alive—we all make differences in the world through our very existence—social intelligence leads us to acquire a basic working knowledge of the principles of social intelligence before we make commitments to work toward preferred goals as historical actors. For example, more enlightened degrees of intention emerge from our improved grasp of social intelligence principles, and we are more likely to achieve our goals when we are practiced in using socially intelligent know-how and strategies.

One of the strongest ways to become deliberate historical actors who focus on improving social class conditions— by reducing or even eliminating some of the destructive consequences of social classes—is to locate and work with others who share a reliable knowledge of social intelligence principles. For example, when individuals and groups concentrate their energies on devising viable strategies to reduce social class ills, we know that their combined efforts will produce increased social justice in social classes and societies more effectively than isolated individual attempts. Our shared authority in these circumstances rests on broad knowledge, high levels of social awareness, and astute assessments of our social situations. Furthermore, we proceed by understanding the complexities and resistance of people who have vested interests in preserving the status quo of existing social classes.

When we work collectively with others toward our shared social justice goals to improve social classes, we need to maintain our individual integrity at all times. The social realities of social classes in their own right—as well as in relation to families, beliefs, cultures, and societies—suggest that we only fully commit ourselves and trust others when we recognize the ultimate transcendence of historical actors' ideals and goals. For example, when we accept vocations to increase social justice by improving social classes, we must at the same time recognize that many people have completely different ways of approaching the same goals in their everyday actions and work.

Historical actors deliberately use historical facts and perspectives to understand their social situations, with regard to their own and others' social classes. For example, when we add historical information to pressing current social facts about ongoing suffering due to social class inequities, we increase our motivation to persist in our social justice goals, and to be truly active historical actors in the present to better serve the future. We use our alertness to past history and history in the making to strengthen our shared momentum to accomplish constructive social class changes during our lifetimes.

Responsibilities

Social intelligence clarifies our understanding of the power and complexities of societies, as well as the ways in which we can make changes that boost the possibilities and well-being of populations. In addition, social justice motivates us to follow moral rationales to guide ourselves and others in constructive directions, such as by limiting or transforming the power and complexities of social classes. Whereas social intelligence prepares us to assume responsibility for the consequences of social classes, as well as delivers strategic goals to improve social classes, social justice ensures that we work more effectively with others to accomplish these complex goals.

We educate ourselves in vital ways when we examine how families, beliefs, social classes, cultures, and societies govern who we are and what we do on a daily basis. Social intelligence allows us to take charge of our lives, and to make commitments to pursue and achieve goals which improve present and future social conditions. We influence our destinies in this way when we concentrate on deepening our understanding of others as well as ourselves, and develop constructive strategies to change the business-as-usual momentum of everyday societies. For example, if we want to create stronger societies for the future, we must make life-enhancing changes in how we organize ourselves and accomplish our most significant goals in the present.

Social intelligence encourages us to define our individual and social responsibilities in the complex mass of social issues that often prevent us from seeing which direction to take. Social intelligence also helps us to pursue social justice in social classes amidst the complex and powerful influences of families, beliefs, social classes, cultures, and societies. For example, in coming to see and understand the restrictive impacts of social classes on the quality of life among less-advantaged majorities in populations, we begin to more fully appreciate the rootedness of social class problems in families, beliefs, cultures, and societies. Incidentally, we often give up trying to improve our worlds when we do not use social intelligence to anchor our efforts, because without social intelligence we necessarily experience these five major social influences as overwhelming and overpowering, rather than as sources of energy and creativity for designing and structuring improved worlds.

We soon see how social intelligence increases the effectiveness of our exchanges with others. For example, we are more successful in articulating and accomplishing what we really want to do with our lives, and at the same time we often become more interested in the ethics of social justice, and what we can do to improve the quality of life in our societies and globalization. We begin to care more about what the world of tomorrow will be like, as well as our problem-ridden present, and we ask more difficult questions of ourselves, such as what our responsibilities for initiating social actions are now.

Because families are the firmest foundation of our socially intelligent knowledge, we think of meeting family obligations as primary responsibilities. However, after we have done whatever we can to meet the needs of our relatives and other families' real needs, social intelligence requires us to make contributions to the common good, so that we live fully and meet our existential needs to both survive and thrive. Furthermore, as we move in these directions, we may choose to go in the socially intelligent direction of honoring social justice as an ideal, which leads us toward achieving more productive goals.

Social intelligence is a pragmatic, secular way to look at ourselves and the world, which may be limited in its capacities to tap into broad religious beliefs. However, social justice also frequently adds depth to personal, universal religious interests in spirituality, such as improving social conditions in different social classes. For example, we work more easily toward universal goals, such as regulating or eliminating the restrictiveness of social classes, when we are motivated by social justice, and when we use social intelligence to define individual and global responsibilities to design practical ways to meet persistent social class needs.

Once we understand emotional systems in our social classes, and build on our historical knowledge of social classes, we create new beginnings in social classes through being deliberate historical actors. Because we are socially intelligent, we are not discouraged by others' resistance to changes in social classes. For example, we know that we can create a greater good for the present and future, and that social intelligence makes us more effective in limiting the destructive influences of traditional hierarchical social classes. Furthermore, we follow social justice ideals in order to transcend our individual and collective setbacks in accomplishing our responsible social class goals.

Conflicts and Losses

When we assess what concerns people most about the quality of their life experiences, we find that they are often preoccupied with the significance of stresses in their everyday activities, especially in lower social classes. When we probe further and ask about the stresses they find most difficult to resolve, they frequently describe how conflicts and losses drain their personal and public lives.

Social intelligence shows us that we need to learn as much as we can about human nature and the emotional intensity of family dependencies, so that we can discern similar patterns of interaction in our social classes and other social spheres such as beliefs, cultures, and societies. For example, we experience conflicts and losses as private individuals in our families, as members of social classes, and as participants in beliefs, cultures, and societies. However, in some respects people may be so caught up in conflicts between and among all social classes that it is difficult to find alternative ways to relate to each other.

Social class experiences—especially from the points of view of members of lower social classes—are often viewed as losses of social class privileges. For example, widespread senses of relative deprivation among members of lower social classes are frequently due to their reactions to losing or not having the advantages that some people in their societies have. Thus, social inequalities drive reactions that produce strong feelings of alienation, as well as conflicts and losses.

When we decide to deliberately nurture our social intelligence, and live according to the principles of social intelligence, we essentially start to create a more level playing field where members of all social classes have opportunities to strengthen themselves and societies by achieving meaningful goals. However, these expansive goals are achieved only when they are founded on constructive social realities. In order to increase social justice in social classes we must establish positive, life-enhancing social conditions by living and working according to the principles of social intelligence.

This trajectory reflects some of the most productive ways in which we can deal directly with our most painful conflicts and losses. For example, when we learn about traditional conflicts between social classes, we are more able to work together productively to establish some of the less popular value choices of equality, inclusiveness, diversity, cooperation, and openness in our private and public relations. We benefit from taking narrow vested interests out of the broad pictures of our lives, so that we work more cooperatively and more openly toward establishing universal social conditions that do not impede the progress of less advantaged individuals, groups, and societies. Similarly, we try to narrow gaps between our yearnings for meaningful lives and the harsh social conditions of members of lower social classes. By so doing we make up—at least in part—for some of the lost opportunities and lost access to resources others have already experienced.

When we move collectively in directions that minimize our shared conflicts and losses, we become more resourceful in accomplishing challenging tasks such as increasing social justice in social classes. Furthermore, as we reduce some of the immediate stresses and suffering in our societies, we make way for working together productively to accomplish global social justice. For example, we deliberately broaden our horizons to ensure that global social class concerns—particularly those expressed as conflicts and losses—are balanced and rectified during our progress toward social justice.

Focusing on dealing with social class conflicts and losses heightens our awareness about the significance of education for improving the quality of life in different populations. However, we should also recognize that social intelligence needs to be a central aspect of new general curriculum planning, if we are to benefit from the most life-enhancing consequences of reducing conflicts and losses in our current social class systems. Social intelligence gives us basic skills to implement social justice ideals in contemporary societies, so that we bring about effective social class changes where both social intelligence and social justice inspire and sustain constructive innovations in social classes.

Fulfillment

Using social intelligence to understand families, beliefs, social classes, cultures, and societies may be discouraging, largely because we discover many complex layers of social realities in ourselves and our societies. Even though social justice gives us real hope for better worlds, it is not always easy or comforting to connect our raw social awareness with visions of better futures for social classes, which include being fulfilled in our efforts to survive and make sense of our worlds. However, social intelligence helps us to see that being fulfilled is a basic existential need. This means that we must pay attention to achieving fulfillment, in the same ways that we direct our efforts toward other preferred social justice accomplishments and developments.

Social intelligence shows us that in many real respects we may not be fulfilled unless we connect our work to change social classes with increasing social justice. Social intelligence not only heightens our awareness of the power and complexities of families, beliefs, social classes, cultures, and societies, but also helps us to create effective social strategies which gradually resolve particular social class injustices. Thus, ideally our socially intelligent orientations create meaningful missions to accomplish, that predictably improve social conditions for all in the present for the future.

Social justice helps us to think clearly about significant local and global aspects of social situations, so that we are more discerning when we make decisions and commitments to pursue particular social concerns like social classes. For example, our attention is then most easily drawn to social problems related to life experiences in different social classes, for example, or to historical national and international turning points—such as wars—that affect social classes in whole populations and the global community. Thus, when we move toward social justice ideals, we use social facts about social classes that we respect and understand through the principles of social intelligence, and gradually achieve more life-enhancing results.

Focusing on social issues about social classes gives us many viable options to improve the present and future for more people in our societies. For example, we may consider that social intelligence and social justice help us to understand more fully how literacy and education improve the quality of life for all people in societies. Consequently, when we work toward goals that create universal access to educational opportunities, we change social classes in crucial ways. We reduce inequalities in educational achievements, increase social class mobility, and gradually control or eliminate some of the traditional social class hierarchies that organize populations in societies and international exchanges.

In order to turn our dreams of increased well-being into social realities, we use social intelligence to design strategies that improve many different levels of communication. For example, we may convince publics of the importance of education for all, or provide better quality education for less privileged populations. Increased international exchanges in education are needed, as well as enlightened professional programs that support socially intelligent social justice initiatives to meet universal educational needs.

IV. Social Classes and Social Justice

Even though we may see some of these connections at the same time that we assume responsibilities to work toward increasing the common good—for example, we understand that improving education reduces some of the most destructive aspects of social classes—we must return to the principles of social intelligence frequently in order to maintain our power and effectiveness in accomplishing such demanding missions or goals. Being aware historical actors helps us to know what we are doing with our lives, which leads us to engage in significant work to reduce the power of social classes, and frees us sufficiently to be fulfilled.

Social intelligence anchors our efforts to accomplish social justice because being socially intelligent makes us aware of the power of the five major non-rational influences of families, beliefs, social classes, cultures, and societies. For example, merely recognizing the emotional dependency of social classes on families, beliefs, cultures, and societies gives us new ways to consider possibilities for generating social class changes. Paying attention to interactions between and among families, beliefs, social classes, cultures, and societies shows us the rootedness of our individual and social problems in social classes, and their continuing impacts on our fulfillment.

V. Cultures and Social Justice

Social intelligence also anchors social justice through cultures, the fourth of the five major social influences that make up the core of social intelligence. For example, cultures reveal socially intelligent values and ideals of societies, which describe and explain the power and complexities of social justice. Cultures also provide intellectual sources that can be used to increase social justice in wide ranges of social situations. In turn, social justice goals offer specific possibilities for changing cultures, which lead us to cultivate social conditions that create and maintain peaceful coexistence among societies and throughout the world.

The reciprocity between social intelligence and social justice in cultures guides our individual and collective efforts to increase the common good. For example, we may start to make use of our social intelligence, by deciding what we can accomplish for others in light of our knowledge about the significance of the five major social influences of families, beliefs, social classes, cultures, and societies. Furthermore, when we recognize how cultures anchor socially intelligent efforts to increase social justice, we still need to acknowledge the continuing impact of interdependence among families, beliefs, social classes, cultures, and societies in individual and social well-being.

A significant part of the process of learning social intelligence, and applying it to cultures and social justice, is to consider cultures as reservoirs of values that represent both constructive and destructive aspects of our civilizations.

Consequently, our responsibility is to identify the most positive links between cultures and social intelligence, in order to use cultures' support to empower the values and value choices of equality, inclusiveness, diversity, cooperation, and openness. These five cultural values in modern and traditional societies or cultures hold some of the greatest possibilities for social problem-solving and reforms that increase social justice.

When we are more discriminating in our value choices, we begin to restructure our cultures and societies in ways that increase social justice. For example, we deliberately choose to honor the values of equality, inclusiveness, diversity, cooperation, and openness so that destructive values are not reproduced as easily in our cultures. Furthermore, moving in directions that restructure our cultures to support social justice requires us to act collectively as historical actors. Thus, we minimize the emotional confusion that results from conflicts and losses in our cultures and societies, and think more clearly about our optimal goals for increasing social justice.

A socially intelligent focus on cultures and social justice keeps us grounded in social realities where meaningful changes in the quality of life in societies and populations are accomplished through being more deliberate in using the values of equality, inclusiveness, diversity, cooperation, and openness. Anchoring our efforts to increase social justice in social intelligence makes a world of difference, because social intelligence provides us with viable means to develop meaningful and effective strategies to accomplish social justice goals. For example, when our tasks are wearying, we replenish our enthusiasm for social justice, by merging ourselves and our thinking with specific cultural resources that inspire us to do things differently.

Socially intelligent strategies hold up well in the long run because of their pragmatic results. They keep our most cherished social justice goals before us, boost our positive commitments to increase social justice, and at the same time yield cultural and emotional resources that help us to take a stand against others' inevitable resistance to increasing social justice. Using cultures as socially intelligent resources makes us more inspired, and yields the emotional determination necessary to persist in our social justice efforts. We recognize tensions within our cultures, but at the same time our cooperative efforts move us closer to the social justice accomplishments we cherish the most.

When we stay steadfast in these directions, we increase our fulfillment, because we realize that we are doing everything possible to create new cultures to support and reinforce social justice. Social intelligence and social justice continue to guide us, so that we increase our commitments to accomplish better futures and rectify immediate social concerns. Our cooperative, open, task-oriented social networks ensure that we get the assistance we need to develop our social justice cultural aspirations in the present for the future.

Emotional Systems

Cultures are made up of social resources that express sentiments and thoughts such as ideas, knowledge, religions, legal systems, beliefs, expectations, ideals, values, morals, ethics, arts, sciences, health issues, and existential concerns. We cannot be human without internalizing cultural and social values, and we are motivated by the dominant values we absorb. From the point of view of social intelligence, social justice is a significant value and cluster of social ideals, which enable us to understand who we are in socially intelligent ways when we pursue our preferred goals.

Therefore, our cultures are crucial intellectual and emotional resources that orient our daily decisions and lifetime commitments. For example, we may decide to live according to the feelings of the moment, or to be as rational as possible in establishing and pursuing daily priorities. Moreover, if we are concerned about particular crises, we can choose to immerse ourselves in new or different cultural values, so that we become more understanding and more enlightened about our complex social situations.

Regardless of the particular aspects of culture that interest us the most, we all benefit from using specific personal or professional values to strengthen our unique selves, or to make more rational value choices about designing and working toward our preferred goals. Consequently, cultures help us to express our subjectivity and objectivity, so that social intelligence guides us in discerning what our options are. Because emotions are involved throughout our decision-making and commitments, it is sometimes difficult to distinguish rational behavior from non-rational behavior. However, our cultures and social intelligence make us more astute in expressing our emotions through our most rational choices, so that we choose our subjective values more thoughtfully.

Given the fact that passions drive much human behavior—including the passion to conform to others' expectations—we benefit from viewing our cultures as emotional systems. For example, considering cultures as emotional systems helps us to distinguish constructive from destructive aspects of our cultures, so that we make more socially intelligent decisions about which values we want to honor and cultivate in our daily actions. Furthermore, social intelligence shows us that our value choices make significant differences, not only in recognizing who we are and what we do, but also in relation to assessing the well-being of others, as well as our ultimate fulfillment from contributing to the common good and social justice.

Once we recognize our cultures as emotional systems, we understand more fully how the vested interests of individuals and groups automatically resist particular individual and social changes, especially those related to the five key dimensions of social intelligence—families, beliefs, social classes, cultures, and societies. All five of these aspects of social intelligence are emotion-driven to some extent, as well as relevant to particular cultures. For example, we may be motivated to persist in repetitive actions that reinforce our shared understanding of the status quo of families, beliefs, social classes, cultures, and societies. Furthermore, it may be only when we suffer from severe disadvantages or deep disappointments from particular social conditions, that we get sufficiently motivated, to bring about positive changes according to the principles of social intelligence, the common good, and social justice.

Both social intelligence and social justice are influenced by the emotional systems of our cultures. For example, when we examine the emotional qualities of our value choices, we become more aware of the discomfort we experience from forging new cultural pathways, or new ways of doing things, by reinforcing less popular values such as equality, inclusiveness, diversity, cooperation, and openness through our actions. People who have upper social class advantages are often reluctant to support the value of equality, and those who like to control others are hesitant to be open and cooperative in their work.

Our socially intelligent tasks do not include taking emotions out of our ways of living and deciding what to do with our lives, but rather encourage us to discover how to invest our emotions thoughtfully in our daily actions. For example, we use our sentiments and feelings to strengthen our efforts to build better future worlds. And we learn how to guide our deepest emotions, so that we find meanings and values that increase social intelligence, the common good, and social justice.

Historical Sources

Historical sources often harbor social facts which define or express our cultures, such as traditional or modern values. Similarly, the objective, factual nature of specific aspects of cultures, such as religions or education, lend themselves to planning better futures, especially futures based on concerns about social intelligence, the common good, and social justice. Historical sources prevent us from becoming mired in emotional trends in diverse social and cultural systems. For example, knowing historical facts about cultures allows us to plan our futures more effectively, because we think more clearly about our options and possibilities for meaningful futures.

Even though the emotional systems of our cultures affect our understanding of history, responsibilities, conflicts, losses, and fulfillment, we gain some control over our emotional investments in particular values by becoming more objective. For example, when we strive to increase our objectivity about the power and complexities of our social situations, we are more rational and thoughtful about our options in all aspects of our behavior. When we concentrate on historical sources of our cultures, try to be historical actors through our cultures, define cultural responsibilities, assess cultural conflicts and losses, and attain fulfillment through our cultures, we reduce our emotional reactivity to cultural challenges in the constant social demands of our daily lives.

Gathering social or cultural facts about histories, responsibilities, conflicts, losses, and fulfillment gradually increases our control over how we act as historical actors in our cultures, especially with respect to social intelligence, the common good, and social justice. We use historical sources to understand how history is being made in the present, and to increase our control over whatever occurs in the future. We also refer to past histories to deepen our understanding of the power of our present cultures, rather than solely to motivate or orient our behavior. However, we need to let go of much of the past if we are to create better cultures today, especially to achieve worthwhile ongoing endeavors like increasing social justice.

Any aspect of our cultures, families, beliefs, social classes, and societies, has historical social facts. For example, we answer pressing current questions by examining how past cultures shed light on who we are today. What do our preferred values represent or reflect through time? What are the most significant trends in current cultures that express specific values and beliefs about education? What differences do historical facts of our cultures make in how we accept or reject particular values today? To what extent do historical facts determine the future of our cultures?

Links between historical facts and historical sources of cultures give us added depth, breadth, and enlightenment to develop our cultures and civilizations. We assess the extent to which we go with the flow of cultural changes in particular periods of time, as well as how we may choose to carve out niches for ourselves with regard to new values or value changes in our cultures. Understanding our cultures more fully also makes us more adept at using cultural and historical resources to our advantage, so that we become more firmly rooted in whatever values we prefer to express in our lifetime vocations or missions.

Thus, cultural historical sources support innovations as well as the status quo. For instance, when we need to enlighten our actions, we gain from immersing ourselves in new values and new cultural perspectives as much as possible. We think differently through social intelligence, and we get clearer about what it takes to create new cultures of social justice for the present and future. In fact, among all five of the major social influences of families, beliefs, social classes, cultures, and societies, cultures have the most dependable historical resources for understanding the past, present, and future of societies. To the extent that we use cultural social facts creatively, our cultures become stronger positive forces for both the present and future. Because we understand social justice differently when we focus on past and present cultural realities, we become more astute in defining particular goals and possibilities.

Historical Actors

Social intelligence, as well as our working knowledge of history, prepares us to be effective historical actors. When we are able to assess significant historical trends and conditions in the emotional systems of our cultures, as well as develop broad views of the history of our cultures, we increase our social intelligence and our understanding of what it means to be aware historical actors.

We depend on social intelligence to enlighten us, in order to formulate meaningful practical goals which lessen our emotional dependence on our cultures. For example, we strive toward building constructive cultures rather than destructive cultures, and at the same time make cultural assets available to as many members of our populations as possible. However, our good intentions are not as significant as our actions, and in order to accomplish constructive cultural goals we ultimately need to work with likeminded others, so that we cooperate to achieve similar ends, regardless of the difficulties that evolve as we move forward.

As long as we depend on social intelligence to guide us, we eventually amass sufficient social facts to support our endeavors. Our knowledge of historical sources of our cultures, together with our understanding of emotional characteristics of our cultures, defines significant cultural and social realities that inspire us to increase social justice in our cultures. For example, we work cooperatively to build cultures to support social justice—by strengthening the values of equality, inclusiveness, diversity, cooperation, and openness—so that we increase probabilities that social justice will thrive and improve populations' qualities of life.

To the extent that we keep in mind the power and complexities of the five major social influences of families, beliefs, social classes, cultures, and societies we put our cultures in broad, meaningful perspectives, which inspire historical actors to aim for increasing the common good and well-being of whole populations. When we are aware historical actors, we envision better present and future social conditions, as well as use particular social realities of the past to achieve success and fulfillment in increasing social justice now.

Social intelligence teaches us that social justice must be supported and expressed by our cultures, if social justice is to be sustained among different societies and globalization. Moreover, we must deliberately build new cultures to support social justice, because this allows us to increase social justice in the long run. For example, both national and international security concerns pose serious challenges, unless we establish broad cultural bases for social justice that allow us to co-exist peacefully with other societies, as well as in relation to dissension and conflicts within our own societies.

In these respects, social justice is essential for our survival and fulfillment. We preserve the best ways of doing things in our cultures, so that our societies will survive. Social justice is not an abstract ideal, but a series of pragmatic goals that we need to achieve through socially intelligent means and strategies. Being an historical actor is also significant, because we need long term views of ourselves and others if we are to create better futures now.

Historical actors develop missions in relation to cultures. For example, we impact our cultures by making long-term commitments to expand social justice, and by sustaining our efforts to increase the common good. We tune in to history-in-the-making when we allow our goal-directed actions to lead us in directions that encourage new value choices. These deliberate actions result in more equality in families, inclusiveness in beliefs, diversity among new social classes, cooperation among cultures, and openness in societies, especially when we apply social intelligence to our efforts to increase social justice. Eventually, social justice values will be more pervasive in our cultures, so that we gradually modify our interactions and exchanges with others throughout our societies and civilizations.

Thus, we gain fulfillment from being agents of social change in our cultures. Being historical actors clarifies our decisions and goals about cultures, so that we deal with our responsibilities, conflicts, and losses thoughtfully. Even though it is not essential to be socially intelligent as we attempt to increase social justice, we are more productive and constructive when we base our actions on social facts. Acting automatically or intuitively does not empower individuals and groups as much as depending on social knowledge and social intelligence.

Responsibilities

Because we continuously use the knowledge and values of our cultures, we must at the same time refresh our cultures with new knowledge and new values. This exchange and reciprocity makes us see our responsibilities differently through our ever-changing cultures, so that we continue to use cultural means to create more ideal present and future conditions. Thus, social intelligence helps us to locate and design more effective ways of being and doing, so that we gradually build better societies for the future in the present.

We are responsible historical actors when we use social resources to envision cultures and societies that support freedom for all people. For example, our ideal cultures may be based on social justice values such as equality, inclusiveness, diversity, cooperation, and openness. Furthermore, we are more likely to sustain responsible cultural goals and actions, when we make deliberate efforts to lead everyday lives according to the social justice values of equality, inclusiveness, diversity, cooperation, and openness.

Our cultures also enable us to define our pasts, present, and futures more decisively as well as more responsibly. The principles of social intelligence help us to realize that the past has gone, and that we need to let go of our most unproductive ways of conducting everyday life. Our present is all we have of the past and future, and we must be as productive as possible in investing our energies in the present, when we aim to increase the common good and social justice. For example, we establish priorities according to our preferred cultural values and ideals, in order to make responsible, accurate assessments of what our social conditions are now, and what they could be in the future.

When we are aware of these possibilities, and assess our priorities in relation to the vast number of cultural choices from which we can choose, we are more socially responsible citizens. Being responsible consists of a series of cultural choices, which gradually bring us closer to realizing our ideals of the common good and social justice. Because cultures show us many facets of current social realities and social conditions, we progress to create satisfying life conditions and results through our actions.

Examples of how we use cultures to express our social justice ideals are seen at different levels of our most significant social experiences. We first learn our basic values from our families and family cultures, and ideally receive a sufficiently deep moral education when we are still young and impressionable, from those who care for us most. Our knowledge of right and wrong guides us to develop our social intelligence, so that we are more discriminating in our value choices about our family interactions and dependencies.

Next, we learn to apply our cultural knowledge to interpreting communities and societies around us, so that we develop and strengthen our understanding of the social realities of families, beliefs, social classes, cultures, and societies. We are who we are in large part because of the beliefs we hold, which motivate us to act on behalf of the common good and social justice. Being aware of our beliefs controls our actions, and we strengthen our intentions to build better worlds by more deliberately selecting or rejecting our beliefs.

Examining our families and beliefs helps us to assess the extent to which our lives are dominated by social classes. For example, although we may not realize the many ways in which our goals are social class goals, social classes still affect our decision-making and assumed responsibilities. Furthermore, unless we select objectives that make us more socially mobile, such as identifying access to desirable societal resources, we may get left behind on the merry-go-round of modern societies. However, we are more responsible when we recognize competing and conflicting social class values, so that we can do something constructive to resolve them through our daily value choices.

In the long run, our cultures may lead us all the way to social justice. For example, when we value social justice in its own right, as well as cultivate values associated with social justice—such as equality, inclusiveness, diversity, cooperation, and openness—we are less likely to be distracted by destructive, individually-oriented, or death-directed values in our cultures. Being cautious and deliberate in our value choices predictably ensures better future cultures and societies for all.

We need to continue to increase the common good in societies, if we are to be responsible in our cultures and timeless missions to accomplish social justice. For example, social intelligence teaches us that we must work productively with others, in order to achieve collective, life-enhancing goals. Therefore, we are cooperative and open with those who support the social justice cultural values of equality, inclusiveness, and diversity that drive our productive actions forward to improve present social conditions for the future.

Conflicts and Losses

Our national cultures require us to cope with wider conflicts and losses than the conflicts and losses in our family cultures. For example, considering conflicts and losses in our cultures and societies involves us in some of the emotional hot spots in our historical, present, and future experiences. When we see the conflicts that make our everyday lives stressful, we more easily define what it means to work toward social justice in our present situations.

Conflicts and losses are more than our personal experiences in our families, although we use our family know-how to understand the seriousness of suffering from intense conflicts and severe losses in societies. Furthermore, unless we learn whatever we can from ongoing conflicts and losses, we will continue to be subjected to stresses that do not allow us to be sufficiently free to pursue our preferred goals. For example, we understand and neutralize our sibling rivalries, in order to transcend their impacts and make constructive contributions to the common good and social justice. To the extent that we replay family conflicts through our everyday exchanges in cultures and societies, we will not have sufficient vision to make optimal changes in how we relate to others, and how society is organized.

Thus, we need to stay alert to the many ways in which we initiate, provoke, or perpetuate conflicts and losses in our cultures and societies. When we are objective about the qualities of our relationships, or our views of others, we prepare ourselves to interact differently, to the point of seeking specific ways to reduce shared conflicts and compensate for mutual losses. For example, by establishing more viable family and social relationships, we create bonds and networks that meet a wide variety of social needs.

Similarly, we benefit from examining our beliefs, in order to identify our ongoing conflicts and losses. If we find that our beliefs do not adapt to our needs, for example, or that losses of good faith cause extreme pain or diminish our will to put things right, we need to get more focused on sorting out what our most meaningful priorities are. This clarifies our beliefs and the beliefs of others, so that we work more cooperatively as historical actors to improve the common good and social justice. Thus, tackling problem areas in our flow of ideas, allows us to design more effective strategies to deal with cultural and social issues that improve the well-being of all.

In these respects, social intelligence helps us to be enlightened cultural leaders, as well as enlightened followers. When we assume responsibilities for our families, beliefs, conflicts, and losses, we develop our capacities to make strategic decisions that improve the quality of life for all. Assuming responsibility also compels us to examine the parts we play in social classes and cultures, so that we use our experiences of conflicts and losses to minimize restrictive social class differences in our cultures and societies.

Recognizing the destructive consequences of conflicts and losses enables us to deal with the damaging consequences of cultures and social classes. How can we continue to support social classes when we see how much energy is trapped in repeating social class conflicts? For example, we benefit from taking our emotional investments out of social class competitiveness and conflicts, so that we see more clearly what needs to be done for the common good and social justice.

We understand the seriousness of the losses experienced by people in lower social classes when we examine our cultures and societies from the point of view of social justice. Furthermore, we close gaps in our understanding when we seek to "put things right" by honoring the ideals of social justice in our decision-making and actions. For example, we decide to privilege the value choices of equality, inclusiveness, diversity, cooperation, and openness in our actions, in order to resolve the tensions of broad social conflicts and social losses.

Our cultures are primary sources of inspiration to bring about individual and social changes that reduce conflicts and losses. We go to our cultures not only to understand the grand dimensions of our shared cultural and societal conflicts and losses, but to find constructive values to repair the damage done in both personal and global contexts. We are responsible for cultivating a high level of awareness about social justice, so that whatever we do will eventually bring about more constructive societies.

We need to assess all corners of our present societies, in order to focus our attention on the damage wrought by our collective conflicts and losses. Who harmed whom in the rough and tumble of personal lives, political pressures, and historical shifts? Where do our responsibilities lie for ending suffering in the world at large? Can we identify social justice as a cultural mission to accomplish when we are socially intelligent historical actors? Social justice is ultimately a practical goal, because creating a greater common good in our world community requires us to work together.

Fulfillment

Much fulfillment flows from exercising our social intelligence and aiming to increase social justice. Whether or not we actually have an impact on social justice matters, but we are not beholden to achieving all the results of our actions before we can feel fulfilled. Although the results of our actions count, in many instances it is sufficient merely to act in directions that increase social justice in order to experience fulfillment, especially when we assess the meaningfulness of our actions in relation to our intentions and social intelligence. Doing the best we can in given situations brings its own rewards.

For example, social intelligence assures us that what we do is based on social facts, and that we generate real hope for better futures, rather than false hope, through our actions. If we consistently use social intelligence as our guide, our knowledge of families, beliefs, social classes, cultures, and societies enables us to achieve our goals in the long run, especially when we work cooperatively with others to increase the common good and social justice. We scrutinize our families to understand more fully the scope and depth of emotional systems in our personal lives, communities, and societies, so that we go forward as aware historical actors who assume responsibilities that deal directly with cultural or social conflicts and losses, as well as increase the common good and social justice.

We do not have to be major local, national, or global leaders to assume these responsibilities. Rather, we move in constructive directions on a daily basis, in order to develop and live up to our potentials as human beings. In the best of all worlds, for example, we may envision that particular life-enhancing changes will occur when masses in populations assume responsibilities for constructive cultural changes, rather than just small clusters of individuals. Similarly, social policies that create relatively equal opportunities for universal education, will improve the social and cultural fabric of societies more effectively, than well-meaning legislation that ultimately merely reinforces existing social classes with harsh restrictions for many members of lower social classes.

Although being responsible necessarily includes strengthening our capacities to work cooperatively with others, we are still individually responsible for our decisions to accomplish our goals on a daily basis. Paying attention to our cultures, values, and ideals is important, for example, because our cultures reliably show us how to envision life-enhancing futures. Value choices—especially opting for the social justice values of equality, inclusiveness, diversity, cooperation, and openness—determine not only our efficacy in reaching our ideals, but also the level of our satisfaction and fulfillment about individual and social situations.

We live fully when we are resourceful in bringing about productive individual and social changes, and when we use social intelligence to guide our missions as historical actors. In many respects, living fully responds to our existential needs, and creates constructive legacies for others. Our responsibilities include caring for our families, as well as nurturing sufficient livable social conditions in communities, societies, and globalization. Furthermore, as we improve situations and possibilities for others, we deepen our fulfillment and capacities to be socially intelligent. Social justice is also more likely to flow from these efforts, for example, because we create better futures for all in the long run.

Dealing effectively with conflicts and losses adds to our fulfillment. No matter how hazardous or difficult our everyday lives are, seeing our situations from socially intelligent perspectives inspires new, more effective strategies that meet needed goals, as well as restore meaning, purpose, and fulfillment to all. Such satisfactions are not imagined, but flow from our increasingly precise efforts to change social facts and given cultural conditions. Even though we predictably experience setbacks in proceeding toward our preferred social justice goals, we can choose to continue to be inspired by social intelligence and social justice, so that we make significant cultural changes.

Our motivations to take responsible actions derive from our cultures and cultural choices. For example, successes in reaching our goals are largely achieved through our value choices and ideals. Being open to cultural guidance enables us to transcend daily difficulties, and to persist in our chosen directions. Furthermore, if all seems lost and we cannot easily surface from the power and complexities of our families, beliefs, social classes, cultures, and societies, we have the option to deliberately choose to re-immerse ourselves in our cultures, so that we find new values that give added meaning to our quests for social justice.

VI. Societies and Social Justice

Societies are a fifth powerful and complex social influence that significantly contributes to our being socially intelligent about accomplishing social justice. For example, in order to increase social justice, we need to use broad social perspectives to understand the societies in which we participate, recognize the ways in which our societies interact in a globalized world, and identify past or present historical forces that propel us into our futures. We ride on the waves of broad social influences, which we need to observe as much as possible, if our future options are to be enlightened and viable.

Broad socially intelligent views of our societies enable us to more accurately assess the varying characteristics of social conditions that exist in our own and others' societies. Comparing different societies helps us to see the extent to which we honor freedom and opportunities for whole populations. Although cultural differences may strike us at first as the most significant distinguishing characteristics of societies, we see that we also need to understand the power underlying cultural contrasts, if we are to be effective in our work as historical actors. For example, we must answer questions about what the most significant shared social characteristics of societies are, and how we can direct changes in societies through time.

In addition, the givens of our current situations include recognizing that unless we try to take some degree of control over them, our societies will automatically change regardless of our preferences. Furthermore, uncontrolled societal adaptations frequently occur in directions we would not choose. For example, when we do nothing to turn the tides of social change in our societies, we predictably reinforce current social inequalities that decrease social justice. Only by deliberately aiming at and achieving social justice, can we create and sustain more constructive social conditions.

Because of these dynamics, we benefit from responding positively to wake-up calls that emerge as we assess our social situations from societal points of view. For example, using broad-based societal perspectives motivates us to establish new value choices and new social conditions in our local and global societies. Only by doing things differently day by day, can we enter into working and living transactions that increase universal access to societal resources and opportunities, thereby creating more fulfilling lives for whole societies. Moreover, even though these aims may be thought of as overly lofty goals, we discover that we can make meaningful differences as soon as we live more deliberately according to social intelligence principles.

Because social intelligence is based on our understanding of the power and complexities of social facts, as well as the dominance of the social influences of families, beliefs, social classes, cultures, and societies, the knowledge and principles of social intelligence guide us to deal with emotional systems in our societies and historical trends. Although a large part of life is a mystery, we can use some meaningful and effective ways to understand where we are in our lives, what we want to accomplish now and in the future, and how to go about achieving our social justice goals. Furthermore, we can depend on social intelligence to both enlighten and lead us in dependable directions, due to our understanding of social facts.

Our fulfillment from going in these directions derives from becoming responsible historical actors who select goals to pursue with others, which increase the common good and social justice. For example, social intelligence encourages us to tackle individual and social problems due to conflicting emotional systems in our societies. These include conflicts and losses of members of our populations who have been overly restricted by cultures and social classes. When we seek to create and maintain level playing fields in our societies, we encourage new value choices that lead us toward social justice through increasing equality, inclusiveness, diversity, cooperation, and openness.

In these regards social intelligence inspires us to make history in our own terms, by focusing on the needs of whole populations. We recognize the limits of human nature, at the same time that we assume meaningful responsibilities to bring about constructive social changes throughout our societies. We act deliberately, so that our values are life-enhancing rather than death-directed, and our goals are constructive rather than destructive. Furthermore, we combine our interests with those of like-minded others, so that we cooperate and work openly toward a practical greater good.

Emotional Systems

Societies are characterized by emotional systems, which are networks upon networks of negotiations and social changes. As communications within and among societies become increasingly widespread in modern times, emotional systems are similarly broader in scope now than at any other time in history. Societal emotional systems are also more intense, due to the depth of shared interests in gaining access to the accumulated resources of prosperous societies. However, because we often see more dramatic interdependence in our family emotional systems, it is useful to make some comparisons between family emotional systems and other social systems.

It is difficult to deny or ignore the intensity of families and broader social systems, because pressures to conform to particular ways of doing things are at the core of both families and societies. However, family interdependence and societal interdependence often differ in intensity when they are placed on a continuum representing a range of degrees of emotional interdependence. Whereas families have dominant leaders, they are expected to nurture all their members. By contrast, societies often meet only the goals of leaders and other powerful people in the emotional systems of societies. Thus, emotional systems in societies reflect the dominance of societal leaders and interest groups, which usually articulate just some of the passions of their populations.

Social intelligence claims that it is because the conforming pressures of emotional systems are so resistant to outsiders, that we find it daunting to deviate from the expectations of families or societies. What we think of as the power and complexities of families and societies may in large part result from their emotional systems. Because it is easier to conform to emotional systems by doing what is expected, it is often not obvious that we can deviate constructively from the assumptions of dominant groups. Thus, we use social intelligence principles to find ways to deviate creatively, because conformity blocks innovations.

Emotional systems in societies include families. However, we are more compelled to pay attention to our families' emotional systems than to societies' emotional systems, because families make more personal demands on our time, energies, and affections. For example, families predictably react negatively to individuals who do not meet their expectations, often pressuring them to conform or leave.

When we examine beliefs and social classes, we find that individuals and groups, who are strongly invested in these emotional systems, try to preserve social order by articulating sentiments—such as loyalty—that support the status quo.

It is more difficult to innovate than to conform to what are essentially the non-rational feelings of others. The emotional qualities of belief systems and social classes take on lives of their own, so that individual participants in these emotional systems feel more pressured to conform than to deviate.

The scope of cultures' and societies' emotional systems is broader than the range of emotional systems in families, beliefs, and social classes, so the impacts of cultural and social systems are compelling in their own right. For example, we are made to feel that we should be up-to-date with cultural trends, or on the ready to take sides about major historical issues that affect our societies. After attacks on our national security we often feel patriotic, and automatically close ranks against outsiders to the emotional systems of our societies and cultures. Consequently, our deep-seated identities with our cultures and societies predispose us to conform even more precisely than usual to their norms and standards.

Because of the degree of intensity of emotional systems in our families, beliefs, social classes, cultures, and societies, we do not consistently conduct ourselves as free agents. However, we predictably restore our clear-headedness when we turn to social justice to guide our day-to-day behavior. This encourages us to refuse to be victims of emotional systems, so that we can pursue the common good or social justice independently. We also try to be objective—or at least release ourselves from the grip of emotional processes—so that we can see what needs to be done for the good of all.

A recurring example of how emotional systems infiltrate our understanding of ourselves and societies is the power of traditions in families, beliefs, social classes, cultures, and societies. Traditions give us a clear sense of what is expected of us in our relationships and social situations. However, when we follow the dictates of tradition, just as when we follow fashion trends, we tend to trade in our deepest thinking and individuality—sources for social justice actions—by conforming to others' standards. Rather, we need to regard trends in traditions with some degree of caution, because traditions often mask inequalities in families, beliefs, social classes, cultures, and societies.

In order to demystify the ways in which societies disguise social injustices, we must deliberately examine and neutralize irrational aspects of societies and social organization. Social intelligence gives us tools to see patterns in behavior for what they are, so that we can declare a clear starting point for increasing social justice. Being objective about social facts increases our responsibilities as historical actors, and makes us more successful in establishing social justice.

Historical Sources

Societies frame social justice concerns because they are our original broadest social systems with lengthy histories of major events and meaningful turning points, as well as emotionally interdependent populations. Record-keeping over long periods of time gives established historical sources power and complexity, by creating substantive roots that connect societies to their social and emotional origins. Furthermore, even though populations tend to record only wars, migrations, deaths, and famines from their earliest stages of development, there is now increased awareness that social conditions—such as relations among social classes—determine many past and present conflicts and losses. Therefore, social histories as well as political histories have significant impacts on defining the present and futures of societies.

Although historical sources of information about societies vary greatly in terms of substance and the amount of information accumulated, artifacts and written records reflect different qualities of societal changes and adaptations over time. Even when information about social justice in past eras is sparse, it can be determined that improvements have been made in how people treat each other throughout history. For example, a continuing momentum in social changes and widespread adaptations defines some of the differences that education and industrial development have made to populations.

We understand societies, and strengthen our capacities to be socially intelligent, by cultivating our awareness of what societies do or do not do for us. Although it is possible to live and die without much knowledge of our social underpinnings, our qualities of life are much improved by understanding the depth and details of our historical beginnings, as well as the values that pushed our ancestors forward to establish our current societies.

Investigating historical sources of our social situations increases the likelihood that we become more responsible historical actors, who use social intelligence to increase the common good and social justice. We benefit from developing social intelligence because it acknowledges the significance of historical sources. Consequently, we become historical actors in the fullest ways possible—by living with purpose and direction in accordance with social needs of the past, present, and future.

Being aware of histories of our behavior also adds depth and meaning to our everyday current decisions, so that we are less emotionally reactive to whatever happens to us. History gives us a particular kind of objectivity, which enables us to think more clearly about the social contexts of what goes on around us, especially with respect to the five major social influences of families, beliefs, social classes, cultures, and societies.

Furthermore, we understand families' emotional systems best when we examine patterns of interactions among family members over several generations, as well as within the particular communities and societal histories of our ancestors' everyday lives. For example, we see the significance of selected beliefs more clearly when we trace our individual and social histories through our beliefs. Furthermore, because beliefs often come into our lives through people rather than through our own volition or decisions, we learn about our beliefs by tracing who made historical impacts on our views of self, others, and the world.

History is also a valuable way to grasp the significance of our social classes, cultures, and societies. In fact, we cannot make sense of these broad powerful social influences without seeing them in their own right, and in relation to each other in different time periods. We order social facts as repetitions in social trends, when we discern how their social and historical conditions have affected our lives. Historical sources are not dead records, but rather roots of life that connect us to the present, and move us to create more productive futures.

Historical sources suggest beginnings rather than ends. For example, when we are at a loss to know how to proceed as historical actors, we refer back to cultural and social knowledge, so that we assess our current value choices with the additional enrichment of further clarity provided by historical sources. Because values are not developed just when we need them, we may consider historical sources of values to discover how they encouraged or discouraged the cultivation of social justice through the ages. Thus, histories of cultures and societies inspire decisions and actions today for socially just futures.

Historical Actors

Social intelligence heightens our awareness about the five major social influences of families, beliefs, social classes, cultures, and societies, so that individuals and groups create effective strategies to increase the common good and social justice. This learning process includes recognizing social facts by accessing historical sources, so that we base our decisions and actions on reliable value choices. It is because we know social facts that we become more effective historical actors, who increase the common good and social justice.

When we try to live according to principles of social intelligence, we stay more closely connected to historical changes in our everyday lives. We see, for example, that all people respond to social conditions, and that some social situations are more stressful and difficult to handle than others. Increasing our social intelligence extends our control over social influences, so that we are clearer about who we are and what we want to achieve.

In some respects being socially intelligent carries us toward social justice. We understand more about the moving forces in our particular situations, when we clear our vision sufficiently to see what we must do to make the world a better place. Social intelligence directs us to take paths that accomplish social justice, and we continue to develop social intelligence as historical actors by pursuing goals that bring about more equality, inclusiveness, diversity, cooperation, and openness.

Our acknowledgment of the importance of historical sources in understanding families, beliefs, social classes, cultures, and societies deepens our understanding of social influences, as well as our commitments to be historical actors. Even though all people in all societies are historical actors, it is only by knowing that we are historical actors that we can act deliberately, with sufficiently strong intentions to increase social justice as well as the common good. We act most effectively when we consider our lives as parts of history that bring constructive social changes into being, through our lived vocations or missions as historical actors.

When we are historical actors, we are no longer content with fragmented personal worlds. We connect our lives to our societies by being responsible for meeting broad social needs. For example, we try to narrow gaps in resources and opportunities between the rich and poor, so that we expand access to societal resources. Our broadened historical views, of who we are and what we can do with our lives, inspire us to assemble social facts that allow more people to benefit from prosperity.

Our missions as historical actors vary depending on how we approach the five major influences of families, beliefs, social classes, cultures, and societies. Ideally, each person becomes more independent in all these social spheres. For example, we become more independent by making commitments to neutralize some of the negative consequences of these influences, while at the same time working with like-minded others to make the power and complexities of these social influences more viable for more people. We use historical resources as historical actors, and find that we can reduce stresses in fragmented nuclear families by connecting them to their extended kin groups. Broadening these emotional networks gives families stronger supports, and guides individual members' decisions or goals more effectively.

Because historical perspectives deepen our understanding of beliefs, historical actors use their most consistent beliefs to deal with difficult social situations. Clarifying our beliefs makes us more effective in formulating goals and applying strategies that accomplish our goals, especially with respect to social justice.

Social intelligence sheds light on social classes in our societies, so that we see more clearly how social class contrasts can be narrowed in significant areas of resources and benefits, such as education. Pursuing universal rights to high quality educations allows us to develop missions as innovators in our societies, so that more individuals and groups are fulfilled through their studies and work.

We also need to appreciate the power and complexity of our cultures in our societies, because knowledge often comes from cultural resources such as ideas, ideals, values, religions, and world views. We immerse ourselves in our cultures to find new metaphors and goals, for example, especially when the going gets tough in choosing cultural goals to accomplish social justice.

Our societies and globalization are the broadest historical influences on social realities and social facts. We draw directly from our impressions of the power and complexities of our societies, in order to envision personal and collective missions to serve the common good and social justice. Furthermore, our successes as historical actors in societies and globalization depend on our understanding of the overall impacts of families, beliefs, social classes, cultures, and societies on our everyday lives and negotiations with others.

Responsibilities

Social intelligence guides us to be more responsible in our thinking and actions, because we heighten our awareness of the power and complexities of social influences as we increase our social intelligence. Even though being socially intelligent includes actions as well as understanding, we depend on the social facts of social intelligence when considering new options. Furthermore, at the same time that we learn socially intelligent principles, we mature in defining our goals and strategies.

Just as it takes us a while to grasp how to apply social intelligence to our everyday lives and rapidly changing social situations, we eventually accept the historical definitions of possibilities that our societies present, and do what we can to make constructive contributions to the common good and social justice. Whereas in past generations our education and lived experiences might not have opened up new possibilities, today we can embrace different historical initiatives to create improved worlds. Our socially intelligent know-how also makes us more responsible in our commitments, so that we are historical actors more fully, as we proceed with our lives and daily business.

For example, using societal and global perspectives to understand our families, beliefs, social classes, cultures, and societies makes us more responsible for the consequences of our actions and commitments. Once we understand the power and complexities of the five major social influences in our everyday lives, we clear our minds to formulate and clarify our visions of what we want to accomplish. This socially intelligent principle makes our aspirations count, so that we understand that whatever we aim to accomplish can happen with both expected and unexpected consequences.

Our general responsibilities for taking care of planet earth start by assuming responsibilities in our families. Honoring our familial responsibilities does not mean that we need to devote all our energies to our families' continuing needs, but rather that we are on the ready to do whatever has to be done to ensure that family members are sufficiently free to live fully. Assessing our responsibilities requires us to assess differences about real and unreal needs, so that we do not inadvertently encourage family members to seek too much comfort through the protection of their families. Rather, the primary task of families is to launch their members—and support them—as they go about their business in the world at large.

We understand our beliefs more fully by examining them from societal perspectives. What do our beliefs signify when they are applied to all members of our societies, or all members of the world community? Do our beliefs reflect and represent social facts? What beliefs would be firmer and more practical for us to hold, given our lifetime experiences? Do our beliefs foster social problems or social justice in societies? How can we become more responsible in our beliefs about societies?

Identifying social classes from societal perspectives is also useful. Although we may have vivid recollections and ongoing close associations with our own social classes, we become more objective about other social classes when we consider the whole range of social classes in societies. To what extent do we support the status quo in societies by staying in our own social classes, or by striving for social mobility? What would societies be like without social classes, or with more equal opportunities for more people? How does our awareness of social classes in societies inspire social justice actions to improve the quality of life for entire populations?

Cultures reveal our ideals and values about societies, and cultural views of social situations help us to be more responsible in our socially intelligent actions. We replenish our motives and energies when we deal directly with the many disappointments that come our way, especially as we strive to accomplish impossible social justice goals which may not appear to make a difference in the short run. Because social intelligence helps us to appreciate how our value choices can turn social situations around, we are motivated to persist in our efforts to bring about better worlds.

The uniqueness of our societies does not get lost in these broad, socially intelligent views of social realities. In fact, we cannot participate fully in globalization unless we hold on to the core of our unique heritages in the midst of our international exchanges. Our countries and civilizations were not created easily or quickly, so realistically we aim to make changes in the long run. We negotiate with others in terms of new social justice value choices—such as equality, inclusiveness, diversity, cooperation, and openness—in order to usher in improved societies and civilizations with more responsible actions.

Conflicts and Losses

Societal and global perspectives are the broadest viewpoints from which to use social intelligence to examine qualitative differences among societies. However, because we are integral parts of our societies, it is more difficult to be objective about our own and other societies. Although social intelligence teaches us how to neutralize our strong tendencies to be ethnocentric, it is difficult to sustain sufficient social distance from our social origins, so that many biases come into play.

In these respects, it is not always possible to reliably assess the conflicts and losses which characterize different societies. For example, we often justify the existence of social problems and restrictive social conditions in our own societies, because we want to maintain what seems to be a safe status quo in the assumptions we make and the actions we take in our societies. However, when we are critical of our own broadest social contexts, we shake the foundations of our understanding of who we are and what we want to do with our lives.

Social intelligence encourages us to see how our societies, and our views of our societies, are based on our knowledge of families, beliefs, social classes, and cultures. These significant aspects of our social networks, and the power and complexities of their social influences, help us to distinguish the most important conflicts and losses that societies experience. For example, examining social classes includes assessing the extent to which major proportions of societies are restricted in their opportunities, as well as who suffers the most from losses during wars, which require us to collect explicit and hidden social facts about fatalities and injuries.

Seeing the broader contexts of our social issues, social problems, resources, and inadequacies sets the stage for contemplating social justice issues more seriously. Although we may not be able to remake our societies in significant ways, we can teach ourselves how to inflict less harm on populations, so that conflicts and losses are minimized rather than maximized. Gathering social facts about societies' social conditions, and aiming to strengthen societies' weaknesses, are basic social intelligence principles. These deepen our social intelligence about how societies work, as well as how conflicts and losses are created or maintained.

Such a plan of action suggests that socially intelligent actions neutralize or even remove some of the most destructive social consequences of conflicts and losses, even though conflicts and losses may be emotion-laden or rigidly resistant to changes. When we understand the power and complexities of families, beliefs, social classes, cultures, and societies, for example, we become more balanced in our assessments of their inadequacies such as conflicts and losses, so that we eventually let go of surplus everyday concerns about these issues. Thus, we are able to focus on thinking how we might best achieve our most responsible goals as historical actors.

Our responsibilities as historical actors include setting aside some of our over-concerns about conflicts and losses within and among societies. We imagine better present and future conditions, for example, which allow us to transcend the impacts of their current conflicts and losses. Consequently, we strengthen our capacities to choose to increase the common good and social justice, rather than extend current conflicts and losses in societies. Furthermore, our new value choices prepare us to reform our societies in socially intelligent ways, so that we gradually attain our preferred goals.

Defining trends in our families, beliefs, social classes, cultures, and societies highlights our starting points for assessing social issues and social problems in societies. We see the emotional underpinnings of these five major social influences at work, for example, when we use social intelligence to reduce conflicts and losses in societies. Even though the emotional interdependencies of social influences and social issues are difficult to unsnarl, they give us pragmatic starting points which clear the way to make effective individual and collective efforts that increase the common good and social justice.

Moreover, our new socially intelligent choices of the social justice values of equality, inclusiveness, diversity, cooperation, and openness make us more authentic as responsible historical actors, who are motivated to undertake specific tasks to reduce conflicts and losses in populations. Our gradual improvements make constructive social changes possible. Consequently, we find others to work with more productively, so that we increase the common good and social justice.

Fulfillment

Fulfillment comes from doing whatever we can to make the world a better place. This fact, which we can all prove to ourselves, suggests that our actions are all-important influences in defining our feelings about life situations, and that empowering our actions with clear thinking is a dependable route to fulfillment. For example, investing our energies and passions in creating social justice leads us in directions that produce appropriate life conditions for more people and more populations. Thus, we develop deep-seated needs to enter into local, national, and global exchanges to relieve restrictive social conditions, and make constructive goals possible for everyone.

Social intelligence moves us toward accomplishing life-enhancing changes by deepening our understanding of the five major social influences of families, beliefs, social classes, cultures, and societies, and orienting our motives and efforts more effectively. Even when we explore only one or two of these major social influences, we change our perspectives about our circumstances, and enliven our actions and intentions. Increasing our social intelligence in these ways expands the common good, and we actively pursue social justice by working with others to establish new value choices such as equality, inclusiveness, diversity, cooperation, and openness.

The five major social influences of families, beliefs, social classes, cultures, and societies draw forth our deepest emotional energies, and we realize that we frequently express our strongest passions through actions associated with these major social influences. These tendencies may allow the five deep-seated social and emotional influences to dominate our lives, or we may free ourselves from them sufficiently to pursue our preferred goals rather than conform to others' expectations.

When we are socially intelligent, we free up our energies to pursue socially valuable objectives, such as increasing the common good and social justice. Furthermore, as we learn more about our families, beliefs, social classes, cultures, and societies, we clarify our visions of possibilities to bring about social changes, as well as our responsibilities to do so.

In these respects our individual and social fulfillment, as well as the legacies we pass on to succeeding generations, depend on our social intelligence and our capacities to accomplish social justice. When we see the potentials and power of different emotional systems, we deepen our understanding of the complexities of historical changes and our roles in them. For example, at the same time that we increase our social intelligence, we improve our abilities to make changes, which culminate in more effective adaptations to broad historical social changes.

Studying our families and others' families is an important first step in grasping the sometimes lethal complexities and consequences that families produce through their emotional dependencies. Our increased understanding of emotional systems allows us to recognize and appreciate emotional dependencies in a wide variety of social networks, which makes us more independent in our thinking. For example, we no longer automatically go with the flow of emotional pressures to conform, but rather insist on thinking independently. Consequently, we clarify our intentions about attaining social justice goals which free others as well as ourselves.

Because our beliefs originate as extensions of our interdependent involvement in our families' emotional systems, we become more discerning in harboring beliefs that expressly help us to achieve our most constructive goals. Similarly, we change our most basic thoughts, motivations, and actions about social classes by modifying beliefs that justify social classes. For example, when we no longer believe uncritically in the advantages of social mobility between social classes, we free emotional energies to make deeper commitments to narrow social class differences, or to reduce the power of social classes in the day-to-day business of our societies.

When we increase our social intelligence, we see connections between our cultures and societies more clearly. For example, we appreciate the social impacts of particular values in cultures, as well as the enduring impacts of historical forces in societies. We realize that the value choices we make inevitably anchor us in repeated patterns of interactions in our cultures and societies, so that we are definitively more or less productive in bringing about improved cultural and social conditions.

Social intelligence allows us to have more options in future societies through our value choices, and participating constructively in our cultures increases our fulfillment in the present and future. When we use objective, socially intelligent views of our societies, for example, we are more likely to focus on goals that increase the common good and social justice. In these respects, social intelligence suggests ways to attain social justice, and prepares us to deal with trials and tribulations that are predictably stirred up by our efforts to gain social justice in problem-ridden societies. Dealing with these major societal challenges ultimately brings fulfillment, as well as productive social consequences like social justice.

Social Justice
Directs
Social Intelligence

VII. Historical Actors and Social Justice

Social intelligence makes us more aware historical actors. We are born into specific historical circumstances, and we increase our historical awareness as we mature. Historical learning is largely governed by our social intelligence, or our capacities to assess present social circumstances in light of the past and future. We are creatures of history as well as social beings. Given the fact that we are inevitably historical actors, because we cannot change many of the basic parameters of our human existence, we can only choose whether or not we want to be aware and responsible given the historical conditions we share with others in our societies and the world community.

Social justice highlights the choices we make as socially intelligent historical beings. When we examine social justice values—such as equality, inclusiveness, diversity, cooperation, and openness—we realize that we can use our socially intelligent principles for good or bad purposes. Social justice is a significant moral choice that we make independently, when we realize that interdependence throughout the world is one of the most significant social facts we must learn and understand. We exist in part to make the world a better place because we can choose to do this. Given the complexities and power of social influences in our lives, it is sometimes difficult to sort out our priorities, which is why social intelligence is a reliable guide to accomplish these ends.

Social intelligence is a skill that teaches us how to handle some of the most non-rational aspects of our experiences as social beings. This is why we can use social intelligence principles to guide us to increase social justice. For example, we are more adept at accomplishing social justice goals, when we control some of our reactivity to the five major social influences of families, beliefs, social classes, cultures, and societies. When we are sufficiently free from the immediacy of pressures to conform to significant others' expectations, we think through more clearly which social justice goals we want to aim for, achieve, and commit ourselves to in the long run. Thus, social intelligence makes us wiser and more responsible because we can predict some of the consequences of our socially intelligent actions.

However, it is often social justice rather than social intelligence that ultimately directs our energies to achieve our preferred goals. In the long run we are motivated to go beyond increasing the common good which we aspire to in being socially intelligent, so that we can increase social justice. We learn that because social intelligence can be used for good or evil purposes, we must be decisive in our constructive moral choices and the positive values we seek to nurture in our everyday actions. For example, socially intelligent awareness is necessary for enlightened social justice action: continuing to increase our social intelligence is a lifetime goal that guides us to make constructive differences in our needy world.

History is a major aspect of gaining awareness through social intelligence, and of using our personal and social resources to achieve social justice goals. Although we can recognize and understand many of the complexities of social influences through applying tools of social analysis, we also have to live directly in relation to historical dimensions of social facts and social realities, in order to take social justice actions in history ourselves. Moreover, it is not enough merely to better our own economic or emotional circumstances.

We aim to become sufficiently independent to lead others toward realizing social intelligence principles and achieving social justice goals. Although this mission can be accomplished in many ways, history is a dependable means to come to terms with social hazards, for example, and to start to reduce some of the ills related to the conflicts and competitiveness in social conditions that result from social class hierarchies. Thus, reducing social class extremes of wealth and poverty is a socially intelligent objective, which ultimately increases social justice locally, nationally, and internationally.

When we are sufficiently socially intelligent to be aware and responsible historical actors, we seize our destinies and take historical actions that impact social change and create constructive social consequences. We develop senses of the flow of history through the past, present, and future, which help us to build individual and social momentums to increase social justice. Social intelligence is our starting point for understanding the formidable social facts which confront us all, and socially intelligent principles keep us on track to accomplish social problem-solving for increased social justice in the present for the future.

Social Action and History

Social action is collective action which is undertaken either voluntarily or involuntarily by individuals and groups in societies. At some level social action is often at least aimed at meeting the needs of populations, even though populations' needs may not be readily apparent, and social interactions may be largely unintentional. For example, social action is essentially the sum total of what individuals and groups do, whether or not this is intentional action. Importantly, societies can be characterized by patterns in their social actions, especially by the ways and means they choose to deal with the quality of life for all members of their populations.

People often react collectively to ongoing historical changes throughout societies in their everyday patterns of behavior. They also react to dramatically changing social conditions, which result from major events such as wars or problematic economies, by trying to adapt to both foreseen and unforeseen circumstances. In any event, whether historical changes are unanticipated or wanted, practical social adaptations are ultimately accomplished collectively rather than by individuals.

Social action includes deliberate collaborative action which is expressed as social policies, political strategies, and planned social interventions. For example, we may aim to increase the common good through much-deliberated techniques, so that we cooperate to achieve shared goals such as social justice changes to social class inequalities. In these respects our collective achievements tend to be recorded in history as social progress, but whether or not this happens, social action may become synonymous with history.

Social action which is less perceptible as history may be significant in bringing about both social and historical changes, because social action is made up of the many value choices of individuals as they conduct their everyday business. For example, when members of populations select values which specifically promise enhanced social conditions, they are likely to produce changes in societies' directions that are conducive to establishing new social justice patterns of behavior throughout their societies. Change happens because new value choices reflect social justice goals, and create new foundations for their societies. Consequently, social actions express equality, inclusiveness, diversity, cooperation, and openness more clearly now.

History shows us that social action is more prevalent and more effective in democratic societies, as well as in societies where individuals believe they can make differences to how social practices are organized and conducted each day. To the extent that individuals make commitments to increase the common good or social justice, their societies become more socially intelligent, as well as more successful in accomplishing constructive social changes. Such actions free members of their populations to be more creative and fulfilled. This sequence of events highlights the social fact that when constructive social action is supported by the masses, new cultures and societies are created, based on nurturing social justice values like equality, inclusiveness, diversity, cooperation, and openness.

Societies that are socially intelligent have more flexible patterns of social behavior and social expectations, than societies which are less socially intelligent and less adaptive to ongoing social pressures. Collective social action in socially intelligent societies supports social justice, as well as invites social innovations and challenges to rigid traditions. Consequently constructive, enlightened social action becomes an historical force in its own right, because it is sufficiently strong to carry civilizations forward in and through these societies.

Societies which are socially intelligent are characterized by aware and responsible historical actors who are willing to commit themselves to take social action that moves history and civilization into better futures. For example, the enlightened social action of historical actors may form social movements in societies. Mass movements are particularly powerful when they have sufficient people to create the critical concerted action necessary to bring about constructive social changes. Social intelligence enlightens the social actions of responsible historical actors, who incorporate social justice values in their social changes. Consequently, this social action may be a catalyst for accomplishing qualitative social changes that improve both present and future societies.

Widely effective social action in societies and civilizations depends on clearly defined leadership and independent free-thinking followers, who want to accomplish the same or similar social justice goals. We serve others when we are socially intelligent agents in social action. Our effective cooperation brings about social changes, because we cannot make widespread qualitative adaptations in societies by working alone. Therefore, it is imperative that we learn how to work with others, in order to create better societies, and improve social conditions for peaceful coexistence.

Historical Motives

Social intelligence makes us more aware of our motives, and increases the meaning of our motives, so that we make more deliberate choices about our goals and values. Using social intelligence in our everyday lives requires us to change our ways of thinking and acting. We do this, for example, when we apply our knowledge of social facts about families, beliefs, social classes, cultures, and societies to selecting our most meaningful motives as responsible historical actors.

When we aim to increase our social intelligence, we foster habits that make us consider historical aspects of our everyday behavior options, so that we more easily connect our present situations with the past and future. We develop historical habits of thought, in order to see more clearly, and more fully, what the real possibilities of our actions are. We realize that history is not merely background noise to our actions, but rather the essence of what we do and what we want to do on a daily basis. Using broad social perspectives of social intelligence allows us to be sufficiently objective in our assessments of our given situations, so that we focus more effectively on our preferred goals and proceed toward them, rather than react automatically to the strongest social pressures we experience in the present. For example, instead of pleasing others, we concentrate on doing what we think we should do.

History is a reliable source of inspiration for socially intelligent individuals and groups. We aspire to understand our historical conditions sufficiently, so that we can focus on staying connected to the past, present, and future. Because our historical motives derive from diverse currents of social changes, our socially intelligent challenge is to advocate and act according to what we believe are the most effective ways to proceed, according to the principles of social intelligence. For example, social intelligence may require us to find the most effective means to provide high standards of education for all members of our populations. With this social intelligence principle in mind, we adapt to our historical conditions by assessing real possibilities for increasing social intelligence, the common good, and social justice in the world at large.

We also find historical motives in the five major social influences that strongly impact qualities of our lives, as well as our fulfillment as individuals and groups: families, beliefs, social classes, cultures, and societies. We help families most by collecting social facts about families' histories, for example, and by understanding what contributions we can make to strengthen families for the future. Social intelligence guides us to draw on our past family experiences so that we nurture productive continuities, rather than focus on repeating past patterns of behavior.

Understanding our personal beliefs, through examining histories of their development in our families, communities, societies, and globalization, enhances our capacities to be more objective in assessing which of our beliefs are most significant for our present and future social conditions. For example, we more easily select or discard our beliefs when we see them in historical perspectives, and act deliberately in relation to historical trends.

History also allows us to view our social classes in meaningful perspectives, so that we understand social justice more fully, and select social justice goals which ring true in relation to current social class conditions in our societies. History records particular social class changes through time, which enables us to assess the usefulness of our present historical motives. For example, we may examine some of the historical impacts of individual and social changes in the social classes of members of the last three generations of our families, as well as in earlier times.

Cultures and societies are additional significant broad social contexts for understanding history and nurturing historical motives. We are more inclined to make commitments, for example, when we see how our actions express our cultures and societies, especially in terms of increasing the common good and social justice. Because history affects civilizations and the world at large, as well as our individual cultures and societies, we need to stay connected to major social trends, in order to motivate ourselves and others to be responsible, aware historical actors in our daily lives.

Agency in History

Conventional curricula for teaching history in schools and colleges often convince us that we lead lives that are separate from history. We may learn many facts and figures about the past, for example, but this knowledge is frequently so compartmentalized and remote in time, that we do not readily apply it to the historical know-how we need to develop in the present, or to solving contemporary social problems now for the future. In fact, history tends to make us feel powerless rather than powerful, due to the sheer mass of historical facts and details that have been accumulated through the ages.

However, in reality it is through history that we experience ourselves and touch the world. For example, we are necessarily historical beings who are inextricably linked to the social conditions of the times and places of our births and life-spans. Furthermore, because we live our entire lives within and among broad historical social contexts, we inevitably respond in different ways to the demands of our particular personal and social or political situations. Our agencies—our capacities to act more or less independently, or relatively free of many of the direct negative influences of major social forces—are our unique responses to our complex social experiences. We therefore benefit much more from choosing to understand our vital historical social ties to others, rather than from denying these significant underpinnings of our being and actions.

Getting to know historical social facts about ourselves and our situations is a meaningful route to creating deep knowledge about who we are. We are not so much a complex mass of people with different personalities, but rather social beings who have different family, cultural, social, and historical heritages. We are integral parts of powerful and complex cultures, societies, and civilizations, as well as collaborators in ongoing historical trends in cultures, societies, and civilizations. Furthermore, because we cannot escape our shared histories and connectedness to others, we benefit from using the principles and tools of social intelligence in our work to increase the common good and social justice. Social intelligence clarifies what our social interdependencies are. Therefore, we are more effective and more fully responsible for present and future social conditions, when we use social intelligence to guide our actions and historical agency.

Paying attention to the power and complexities of the five social influences of families, beliefs, social classes, cultures, and societies heightens our senses of agency, as well as the agency of other individuals, groups, societies, and globalization. Because our social intelligence depends largely on our understanding of families, beliefs, social classes, cultures, and societies, we gradually learn how to make more discriminating choices in accepting or rejecting ways of seeing the world, and how to act in light of the common good and social justice. Ultimately, our imperative existential needs to be meaningful and effective historical actors, in order to live fully, move us forward to create better worlds through our actions.

When we consider some of these different aspects of historical agency seriously, we realize that above all our unique agencies are expressed as the sum total of the options we select in conducting our daily lives. For example, our value choices lead us to act or not to act in given situations, which is why being socially intelligent is synonymous with preparing ourselves to be effective in accomplishing social justice goals. We choose to express social justice values such as equality, inclusiveness, diversity, cooperation, and openness, so that we more easily establish social conditions that increase social justice for all.

In sum, we choose to deliberately develop our historical agencies in order to be true historical actors, who make deliberate differences to our civilizations and globalization, as well as to our communities and societies. We strengthen our social awareness and capacities to make constructive value choices, so that we go forward to discover and implement social justice through applying social intelligence principles in our decisions and actions. Fortified with a deep knowledge of who we are, what we want to contribute to societies, which goals we need to accomplish, and which commitments we should make, our lives take on new shapes and increased vitality to continue our social justice work.

Historical Consequences

All our actions have consequences, whatever the intentions of our actions are. Also, whether we function fully as historical actors with a strong sense of agency or not, we often stir up consequences that are both fairly easy to delineate and difficult to identify. Understanding that our actions necessarily have historical consequences increases our responsibilities for our actions, and we become more in charge of both the intended and unintended consequences we produce in difficult social situations.

When we choose to examine the grand scheme of things in our worlds, we discern cycles in patterns of changes in wide ranges of social circumstances. These regularities increase our capacities to explain or predict behavior. However, regularities in vacillating periods of unrest and calm often change rapidly, especially given the power and relentlessness of social influences. Thus, we cannot be certain about what all the consequences of our actions are, especially when some historical results occur in far-off futures.

Being socially intelligent prepares us to be historical actors who make long term historical decisions and commitments. For example, when we are socially intelligent we do not try to reform educational institutions before we have established a fairly sound working knowledge of current educational practices and needs. As historical actors, we use this social knowledge about the possible historical consequences of our actions, to assess whether or not we want to advance the cause of social justice in particular educational circumstances. In the best of all worlds, we move forward through our historical agency to create improved, socially just conditions for education.

One of the easiest and most accurate ways to predict what historical consequences are, is to examine our families' histories over several generations. When we have sufficient historical information about our families, we create a time frame of the past two hundred years as a starting point to trace past family trends to the present. This allows us to assess, for example, to what extent particular family members did well in our families and communities. Who lived the longest and had the most successful outcomes? Who were the most central players in our family relations? Whose children lived or died? Who raised their children with help from their kin group?

Our beliefs also have historical consequences, especially because our beliefs come to us initially through different family members: our most important beliefs are usually passed down by our closest relatives rather than others. Furthermore, we tend to absorb relatives' and ancestors' strongest beliefs without knowing it. In these respects our beliefs are both functional and dysfunctional historical consequences of being located in particular places at specific times, unless we deliberately choose our own preferred beliefs now.

Similarly our social class experiences have histories. We are often historical consequences of others' social class interactions, particularly when we continue to share the same social class memberships. Although we may seem to be historical accidents as we grow and develop, we can turn our trajectories around and become sufficiently free to challenge and reverse some of the power and complexities of the social class memberships we had from birth to the present.

The social and historical consequences of the cultures we belong to are additional powerful, complex influences on who we are and what we want to accomplish with our lives. We need to stand up to the many challenges involved in changing historical consequences in our cultures, if we are to be sufficiently free to create more constructive long term cultural goals for our futures. When we put aside the fact that our past may determine our present and future, we increase our agency sufficiently to move ahead with our preferred goals, rather than stay stuck in historical consequences.

Lastly, whether we consider our societies to be tragedies or oases, cultures and societies are also historical consequences. Both our worst cultural problems and our most supreme social ideals express the historical consequences of others' previous actions. Incorporating history in our socially intelligent views of the world, makes us aware of the extent to which we allow ourselves to get trapped in the most crippling networks of historical consequences of deceased others' actions.

Social intelligence helps us to appreciate the power that these historical roots have over our capacities to be sufficiently free to create viable life conditions. We need to release ourselves from historical consequences, because otherwise we restrict our resources to invest in the future today. We do this by inviting social intelligence and social justice to guide us in beneficial ventures, which help populations to thrive in more constructive social conditions. We necessarily put some historical consequences to one side, in order to progress decisively toward more peaceful futures based on equality, inclusiveness, diversity, cooperation, and openness.

Present and History

We understand our present best when we have a working knowledge of our history. However, we cannot consider only our own histories when we take action in the present. Because so many complex influences impact our social situations, we need to absorb the present for what it is, without immersing ourselves too deeply in what has already passed. When we aspire to increase social justice, we must come to terms with the present as fully as possible, in order to realize better conditions now and for the future.

Our present is an extension of the past, and yet the immediacy of the present makes it potentially different from the past. Because we are not completely sure of where we are going in the present, we have a strong sense of possibilities for the present that are not directly related to a past that is already lived and gone. Therefore, because the past is more static than the future, we cannot cling to the past productively. We need to learn from our past successes and errors, and at the same time move on in the present.

Discontinuities between the past and future give us stronger senses of freedom than looking closely at a past that seems so powerful that it could determine our present situations. By unhinging our connectedness to the past, we more easily enter fully into whatever the present brings, especially in terms of contributing to the common good and social justice. This makes us more empowered and more interested in taking new actions in the present, so that to some extent we change what has happened previously in our societies and civilizations.

Social intelligence helps us to clarify our understanding of the mutual impacts of the present and past. It is not so much that we yearn for a present that is like the past, or that we want continuity with the past, but rather that the past gives us some useful roots and rootedness for the present. Our present moorings may be more secure when we stay connected to our past, for example. In fact, there is a sense of importance or depth about staying connected to the past, because we find that when we do not acknowledge our ties to the past, we may wither and die, or at least not produce the free-flowing energies necessary to be truly vigorous in our present accomplishments.

Because social justice extends our social intelligence work, we further refine our intentions and commitments to improve social conditions in our worlds, when we stay connected to history in meaningful ways. For example, nurturing social justice enables us to focus our attention on problem-solving in the present, so that we gradually let go of destructive connections to difficult pasts. When we are motivated by social justice we use social intelligence to better our social conditions now, rather than yearn to make the past right today when it is finished and cannot be changed.

Social justice enables us to revere the past sufficiently, so that we do not discard our heritages, but rather use them wisely in the present. We do not need to get rid of the past as much as to refine past influences, so that they are positive for all in the present. Thus we retain whatever is useful from the past, in order to deepen our commitments to work effectively in the present, and bring social justice values into being. For example, we deliberately choose equality, inclusiveness, diversity, cooperation, and openness so that we learn from our past experiences, and create new kinds of immediacies and priorities in the present.

Social justice is a present goal in relation to whatever our past experiences were. When we deal successfully with past problem areas in our families, beliefs, social classes, cultures, and societies in new present circumstances, we often reduce many difficulties we may have wrestled with for our lifetimes. Furthermore, when we are responsible historical actors, we can trade past ills from our early experiences for new attitudes, decisions, and actions in the present. These changes suggest more possibilities in the present than in the past, so that we create and maintain constructive momentums to go forward to better futures.

Many of our present energies are based on ideals and values which we learned in the past, but could not use successfully until now. Social intelligence helps us to mature, for example, so that we take our past experiences and distill them, rather than discard them, which allows us to start anew and continue to pursue our preferred goals in the present. We are freer because we are no longer tied to an unproductive past, and social intelligence gives us broad perspectives from which to assess new, real, responsible possibilities with regard to present concerns about social justice.

Future and History

Social intelligence needs to be directed toward achieving constructive rather than destructive goals for societies, civilizations, and self. Although hypothetically social intelligence is accumulated practical knowledge and know-how that can be used for infinite purposes, including both good and evil goals, the emphasis in *Social Intelligence and Social Justice* is clearly placed on applying social intelligence to increasing social justice. When we look at the broader pictures of our lives—a basic routine in practicing the principles of social intelligence—we need to remember that history and social intelligence give us knowledge not only about how to deal with the present, but also about how to prepare improved futures for all.

In this section of *Social Intelligence and Social Justice,* **Social Justice Directs Social Intelligence**, we see that aiming to increase social justice is one of our most practical and beneficial ways to make productive use of social intelligence. In these respects, social intelligence is merely a means which is best used to achieve social justice goals, a topic which is discussed more fully in the next chapter of *Social Intelligence and Social Justice.* Nevertheless, social justice achievements and outcomes also benefit from applying strategies that are enlightened by social intelligence. For example, socially intelligent goals are more thought through from long term perspectives, and therefore more enduring, than if individuals or groups band together to accomplish social justice without the support and guidance of social intelligence.

Social justice directs social intelligence so that we learn from past and present social conditions how to create or manage improved futures. History, which incorporates vital social facts about the past, present, and future, guides and sustains us in building social intelligence, so that we face forward realistically in order to achieve social justice. However, the moral ideals of social justice alone are not sufficient to ensure that we can take our best aim to accomplish social justice. For example, social intelligence steers us clear of the limiting and restrictive effects of the five major social influences of families, beliefs, social classes, cultures, and societies, so that we make progress in building civilizations and societies which provide improved social conditions for all members of their populations.

Nevertheless, it is particularly social justice and the future that inspire social intelligence to create new designs in opportunities and life satisfactions for both traditional and modern societies in the long run. Although we will always have to pass on to our children and new generations the knowledge of how to use principles of social intelligence and social justice to organize our future societies and globalization, these are attainable goals because we can learn and teach them. We are not doomed to fail in creating more viable societies in the future, but rather inspired to keep trying to accomplish what we know is possible and beneficial. We are not perfect human beings, but we can do better than we have been doing in organizing our resources and fair practices.

In some respects, we can depend on members of our youngest generations to produce better worlds now than we have done historically. We live by using social intelligence, whether we realize this or not, and when we are more deliberate in increasing our social intelligence, we are more responsible historical actors and more likely to accomplish social justice and improved futures. This social fact inspires young adults, especially those who are ready to take on the world as they achieve adulthood. It is also rewarding to teach young adults principles of social intelligence, because they are often ready and willing to go forward confidently into the future with these useful tools and skills.

Our legacies include efforts to create more fair societies for the future. As participants in globalization, we see the enormity of the tasks involved in forging and sustaining world communities. A social intelligence principle is that human beings can overcome immense obstacles, as well as improve how they think, act, and make commitments. Because our identities as socially intelligent, responsible historical actors motivate us to maintain world views that envision better future worlds for all, we do not hesitate to meet our existential challenge of increasing social justice.

VIII. Social Intelligence Means to Social Justice

Social intelligence is best used as a means to accomplish social justice, rather than as an end in itself. When we concentrate only on staying socially intelligent, or on becoming more socially intelligent, we in fact are not as socially intelligent as when we habitually view and assess the world at large on a continuing basis, in order to make universal constructive contributions. For instance, social intelligence calls into question the quality of the societies we produce, so that we are compelled to be critical and active in deciding what it is we want to do with our lives, and how we want to accomplish social justice for all. Resolving these existential issues increases our motivations to be responsible historical actors who make commitments to pursue social justice.

The relationship between social intelligence and social justice—the dependence of social justice on social intelligence to accomplish enlightened goals—suggests that in order to have meaning, purpose, and direction in our actions, we must eventually transcend the social fact principles of social intelligence, so that we reach beyond what exists in our troubled worlds toward social justice. Furthermore, because social justice is a cluster of related ideals, social justice is particularly pertinent for guiding our socially intelligent efforts to create new and better worlds today for tomorrow, which helps us to be more successful in accomplishing social justice now.

Because social justice is often best accomplished through using social intelligence, we can assess the overall strengths of social intelligence in inspiring social justice, by breaking social intelligence down into the most significant social facts about the five major social influences of families, beliefs, social classes, cultures, and societies. For example, we scrutinize social facts about families, beliefs, social classes, cultures, and societies, so that we can be more discriminating in our efforts to accomplish social justice directly and effectively.

Although our focus needs to be specific in understanding whatever it is that is most distinctive about families, beliefs, social classes, cultures, and societies in relation to social intelligence and the accomplishment of social justice, we must also discern how families, beliefs, social classes, cultures, and societies interact with each other, in large part to ready us to work with others to attain social justice goals, or at least to identify how social intelligence helps us to increase social justice. For example, we cannot consolidate strategic means to make our efforts truly instrumental, unless we steady our aim for social justice, as well as move reasonably slowly and carefully to this end.

Social intelligence is a way to improve our effectiveness because it points out our human frailties, and suggests ways to act on our strengths rather than our weaknesses. For example, we need to be able to appreciate emotional interdependence in families before we try to combat false beliefs, harmful social classes, dangerous cultures, or lethal societies. Social intelligence helps us to see not only what is characteristic of these five major social influences, but also how these influences interact together to impact entire populations. Unless we do this, we may be too easily duped into believing that we are reforming social conditions when we may merely be reproducing societies with as many or more social problems and social issues as before.

Being socially intelligent about our families, beliefs, social classes, cultures, and societies encourages us to be more willing, responsible historical actors who make commitments to produce and share the common good with others. No particular major social influence alone has strong effects on us, but rather the workings of all five major social influences impact our lives. We are who we are, and we do what we do, largely due to the power of all five of these major social influences.

These influences also increase our objectivity in assessing their restrictiveness on possibilities and opportunities for all. For example, because we are so used to being in the presence of families, beliefs, social classes, cultures, and societies, we usually take them for granted. Consequently, we are not sufficiently critical about these social pressures, largely because we do not want to upset the status quo of our communities and societies. However, at the same time that we essentially decide to keep things as they are, we neglect to address pressing social justice issues, and allow unfairness to be perpetuated or increased.

Families as Means

Families are the first dimension of social intelligence to consider when viewing social intelligence as a means to accomplish social justice. Families are significant sources of social facts, which illustrate some of the most vital characteristics about human nature and human functioning. For example, people may be so much under the sway of their interdependent family relationships, that they do not consistently act freely or in their own interests. Social intelligence is a complex, composite concept which clarifies our understanding of the extent to which we are in charge of our lives, and the extent to which we conform to others' expectations.

Only after we sort out our priorities through interacting with significant others, especially our closest family members, can we make progress in formulating realistic socially intelligent goals. For example, we start by identifying and consolidating our social intelligence, so that we firm up these foundations for building more social intelligence. When we have sufficient social intelligence, we become aware historical actors, so that we pursue social justice more ably in our everyday work with others. We benefit from continuing our family interactions along these lines, because we cannot direct our actions toward social justice effectively without using social intelligence.

So what is it about families that reveals the nature of human nature, so that we can predict more easily and more reliably how to intervene effectively in other human relations? How does participating more deliberately in personal family relationships give us the freedom to meet our families' needs and pursue social justice goals? How are our closest emotional relationships tied into how we work with others, and whether we live peacefully with others? Can we be objective about the intense dependencies in our families, so that we understand ourselves and our relatives better, as well as people who live in varied international cultural and social settings?

Families help us to see and actualize our human potential as well as others' potentials. For example, when we examine patterns in family interactions, family conflicts, or family estrangements, we gain a deeper understanding of the interdependencies and needs that push people to react to each other, rather than to think through what should be done in particular situations. Even though some families are divided or broken, there continue to be ways and opportunities to change established patterns of family behavior, so that their wide ranges of family needs are met. We also have responsibilities for those who cannot yet work toward making constructive changes in themselves and their families.

When we laboriously build knowledge from social facts about our families, which include family histories over several generations, we discern more of the power and complexities in family dependencies. These postures and practices prepare us to be more critical about how we behave and negotiate the most intimate aspects of our lives, which ultimately helps us to meet challenging responsibilities to increase social intelligence, the common good, and social justice. We increase our objectivity through learning more social facts about our social situations, and consequently, our social justice efforts benefit others as well as ourselves.

Going beyond our own family experiences, by understanding national and international family trends more fully, moves us in directions of strengthening the foundations of our social intelligence and achieving social justice. We cannot scrutinize our family needs only, however, if we are to increase the quality of family circumstances in entire populations—one of the goals of social justice. When we are responsible historical actors, we use our knowledge of families in many varied social situations, especially to grasp more fully what people value and need in order to coexist peacefully.

Trying to understand local and global families is a valuable way to deepen our social intelligence, as well as to think clearly when we negotiate with significant others, whatever those negotiations may concern. We become more socially intelligent from steeping ourselves in family knowledge, and as a result we are more effective historical actors in expanding the common good and social justice. Consequently, our progress in using social intelligence, as a means to accomplish social justice, starts with understanding what is really going on in our families. Seeing how families resist their members' attempts to innovate, or how families prefer to maintain the status quo, allows us to feel the power of families' non-rational reactions, even to their insiders' attempts to introduce new or improved ways to do things.

Beliefs as Means

The second dimension of social intelligence, beliefs, is a significant means to accomplish social justice, because our beliefs motivate us as well as clarify or distort the social realities of our particular situations. For example, when we pay close attention to what our beliefs are, we can begin to nurture more constructive beliefs that help us to attain social justice.

Choosing primary beliefs to direct our actions is crucial in making social intelligence a means to accomplish our social justice goals. When we are objective about discovering our innermost beliefs, and assess them for our deepest purposes, we gain more control over our destinies. Rather than accept our beliefs as integral parts of our human nature, we see how to challenge and change our beliefs, so that we more deliberately choose what our motives and outcomes are.

The process of selecting our preferred beliefs is not easy. First we must recognize what beliefs we hold, especially because some of our most cherished beliefs are often hidden. It is usually easier to be objective about our peripheral beliefs than our deepest beliefs, because our deepest beliefs function as integral aspects of our identities and were acquired in our earliest childhood years. Also, a reason why it is very difficult to change our deepest beliefs is that they are inextricably tied to our family dependencies. Consequently, making adjustments in our beliefs is often perceived by us and others as threatening ourselves and the well-being of our families. For example, our basic beliefs about women and men may have direct impacts on our families' structures and ways of doing things, especially when these beliefs shift through time rather than stay neatly in place.

Assuming that we are bold and courageous in changing our beliefs, so that we move away from our initial programming in our families which incorporated relatives' preferred beliefs for our adulthood, we are predictably subjected to pressures from our families to change back to our original beliefs. These pressures range from relatives' communications of mild displeasure, to family members uniting against our innovative beliefs, with the result that it is impossible to interact in our families as usual. In extreme cases, whole families may shun individual family members who make dramatic shifts in their beliefs, with the result that those who change their beliefs no longer have access to significant family members or family events.

Increasing social intelligence, by modifying our original beliefs, is usually disconcerting, daunting, and difficult. Because being socially intelligent means little to most people, individuals' attempts to reorganize their beliefs often appear to others as random, arbitrary, or mischievous. However, rather than go back to our former beliefs, which merely reinforce the status quo in our families and societies, it is more socially intelligent to persist in clarifying our beliefs, so they assist us more productively to accomplish social justice goals.

Sometimes our beliefs are entwined with clusters of religious beliefs, which makes this process of editing our beliefs more treacherous. Nevertheless, we can usually maintain authentic religious beliefs by practicing them differently, especially when our original religious beliefs do not support social intelligence and social justice. This decision is not anti-religious, but rather puts individual maturity and discretion ahead of staying loyal to families' ways of doing things, worshipping, and observing religious ethics.

Beliefs are important to social intelligence and social justice because whole populations can be moved to act according to particular beliefs. For example, strong beliefs in traditions may slow the progress of science, just as beliefs in science may override some of our beliefs in the sanctity of human nature. Even though broad social influences of beliefs and trends in beliefs affect us differently, beliefs need to be considered seriously in our strategies and commitments to pursue social intelligence, the common good, and social justice.

Sometimes our pathways ahead seem impossible to take, given the obstacles that beliefs evoke. However, social intelligence guides us to have faith in the social fact that moving in a particular direction gradually changes our behavior as well as the actions of others, so that the world changes itself gradually. All we need to do is face in constructive directions such as social intelligence, the common good, and social justice, so that our long term efforts are better coordinated with the work of like-minded others. Our collective actions then empower our intentions and results, so that real and substantial modifications are accomplished in spite of the odds against this possibility.

For example, at best social intelligence may lead us to make productive commitments about beliefs in education. We learn more about how education helps us to think differently, so that we are better able to control ignorance and its negative consequences. One of our aims as historical actors is then to create communities that inspire individuals and groups to increase social justice in education through socially intelligent means.

Social Classes as Means

Social classes, the third dimension of social intelligence, are another means to reach social justice through social intelligence. When we consider social classes, we include concerns about social inequalities, economic inequities, status differences—according to criteria such as race, ethnicity, gender, sexual orientation, religion, education, and ablebodiedness—and the growing disparity between upper and lower class resources and opportunities in modern industrial societies.

We often become aware of social classes when we are children, but then we usually have little appreciation of the significance of social classes, or of how social classes set up different groups of people for unequal living situations, sometimes for many generations. Social intelligence is necessary to develop a full understanding of the harsh realities and pernicious social consequences of social classes. Moreover, seeing connections between social intelligence and social justice is crucial for making changes in social class structures, cultures, attitudes, and behaviors.

It is difficult to win the hearts and minds of people sufficiently, so that they are interested in changing social classes in order to be more equal. Sometimes, with very little real knowledge of social classes, individuals and groups act on bases of social class interests, but rarely do they want to reform or transform social class roots in societies. Rather, most people are satisfied to invest their energies in becoming sufficiently socially mobile to provide their children with access to more resources for the next generations. However, if only social mobility occurs, these individual and social motives have merely reinforced the status quo, so that social classes either reproduce themselves or develop more marked contrasts in resources and opportunities.

Social intelligence makes us aware of the injustices involved in conventional social class exchanges, and inspires individuals and groups to make commitments to changing social classes. For example, socially intelligent historical actors may implement initiatives to educate members of lower social classes, so that these individuals and their families have more job options. Educating members of lower social classes also helps individuals to connect their increased opportunities with goals that continue the work of social intelligence and social justice.

When social class distinctions are not based on clear-cut differences like resources—for example, social classes based on ethnic contrasts—it is often more difficult to be knowledgeable and critical about social class hierarchies. In fact, the unfairness and arbitrariness of ethnic social class distinctions may lead more readily to extra striving for social mobility, in order to ease the immediate pain of having less social status, rather than to reforming or eliminating social classes. Social intelligence is an important intermediary goal in this situation, because one purpose of social justice is to heighten people's awareness of injustices, so that more universal improvements in social conditions can be achieved.

Another dividend of increasing social justice through social intelligence and social classes is that we become more concerned about the competitiveness underlying social class structures. For example, when populations value and practice cooperation rather than competition, they make value choices that transcend the acquisition of material goals that dominates social classes in modern societies. Social justice values such as equality, inclusiveness, diversity, cooperation, and openness allow us to prosper in societies that relinquish at least some aspects of the competitive foundation of hierarchical social classes.

Perhaps the single most significant value and policy choice, which could lead to major changes in social classes, is to expand high quality educational opportunities within and among populations, especially in less developed societies. New, stronger societies are more likely to be built when ignorance is dispelled, and particular educational goals—such as equal opportunities for all—become realities rather than dreams. Consequently, when the common good and social justice are attained through socially intelligent social class changes, our improved present and futures are more assured.

Social classes reflect shared inclinations to conform in human behavior, but they need not determine our futures. Social intelligence helps us to see social classes as human creations, most especially for division-of-labor survival purposes in the distant past. However, countless generations have now learned many different ways to survive, and social classes are no longer necessary for the satisfactory functioning of societies, even though we may still appear to be largely dependent on social classes in our current ever-expanding social worlds. One of the challenges of social intelligence is to design new ways to organize societies, so that social justice thrives and is not sacrificed to social class vested interests, as we learn how to co-exist peacefully.

Cultures as Means

Cultures make up the fourth strand of social intelligence in that the values, ideals, expectations, norms, knowledge, and national laws of cultures influence how individuals and groups act on a continuing basis. Furthermore, the content of these aspects of cultures directs us to make value choices, and shape the cultures of civilizations. For example, we are who we are in large part because of what we value, and due to the meanings we attribute to different facets of what we do on a daily basis.

Thus cultures orient us toward particular paths of conformity or deviance. The substance of our societies is usually found in patriotism for instance, which often expresses those values which most directly reflect the views held by the majority of leaders or people in our societies. Similarly, different religions within and among societies reflect clusters of widely shared values in their cultures, so that selected global values become bases of civilizations as well as societies. Because cultures are not static, and may not even be stable, they frequently initiate social changes. Values are significant means that individuals and societies use to promote and adapt to rapid social changes such as population trends, migrations, and globalization.

Social intelligence makes us more aware of the power and complexities of our cultures, and the relationship between our cultures and societies. In some respects we usefully think of cultures as having at least the potential to form new kinds of societies, even though historical changes continue to impact the substance of our cultures and societies at all times. When we try to understand ourselves and others more fully, for example, we see that cultures highlight societies' contrasts in perspectives and world views, so that we must increasingly account for the cultural underpinnings of our everyday lives, if we are to face up to the social facts of our particular situations.

Social intelligence increases our cultural choices. When we are socially intelligent we no longer automatically accept our cultures as they are, but rather question the many ways in which we can create new cultures for the present and future, as well as accept those parts of our cultures that we want to continue into the future. In these respects, our cultures often have more significance for the qualities of our lives than our ongoing social contexts, because cultures determine dominant characteristics of the social conditions and emotional climates that create and perpetuate our societies.

One of the cultural choices that cultures give us is to decide how we define constructive and destructive aspects of our cultures, as well as cultures which support life or lead to death and destruction. Besides understanding differences between cultures which support collectivities or individuals, cultures may threaten or sustain our wills to live and coexist peacefully. Cultures are often our best human answers to questions about whether or not we live and thrive, as well as to questions about assessing human possibilities and responsibilities.

Not least, cultures help us to see why we need to be interested in developing our social intelligence, contributing to the common good, and increasing social justice. When we are knowledgeable about the social conditions of our societies, we see that a reason to stay alive is to create better societies for the present and the future. Because cultures help us in this endeavor, they become essential means to achieve social justice goals.

One of the most worthwhile goals to aim for in increasing social justice is to define and act on new value choices. For example, emphasizing less popular values like equality, inclusiveness, diversity, cooperation, and openness opens doors for new possibilities. These forward looking preferences orient us toward daily value choices that support new cultures and new societies, and increase opportunities for all. Therefore, our cultures show us how to design new futures and create opportunities to attain new goals.

Social intelligence is a means to achieve social justice goals, because we use cultural knowledge to actualize our informed dreams of what societies and futures can be when universal needs are increasingly met. Cultures are particularly significant aspects of social intelligence, as well as critical means in our enterprise to improve social conditions. For example, we refresh our frustrations and weariness by immersing ourselves in cultures, so that we can continue to work with others as historical actors. Our concerted efforts include using cultures to increase social intelligence, the common good, and social justice, in order to ensure improved futures for all.

Societies as Means

Societies are also means to reach social justice goals. Societies are the fifth, broadest dimension of social intelligence that helps us to put our individual lives and social justice in perspective. Consequently, societies help us to be more objective about our social realities, and more practical in aiming to increase social intelligence, the common good, and social justice. Without the breadth of vision of societies, it is difficult to assess accurately the universal needs populations have, and the courses we can take to achieve social justice.

When we assess our personal troubles from the more narrow points of view of individuals and communities, for example, we often lose sight of the greater good, and tend to exaggerate the intensity of crises in our own limited social situations. However, taking a step backward to see the broader pictures of our lives soon checks our inclinations to be drowned by our subjectivity, or too focused on our ethnocentric urges.

When we realize that we are members of societies, we are reminded of stark historical trends and historical social realities, which compel us to be more critical and more objective about our priorities as we go about our daily routines. In these respects, societies awaken us to wider truths that inspire our actions and commitments. Consequently, we work toward social justice more effectively and more purposefully, because we now aim to meet more universal needs.

We can also see how societies are means to understand who we are and what we should do with our lives in relation to evolution. Are we instinctual animals, or can we rise above our animal origins by striving to accomplish social ideals like increasing social justice? What is our basic human nature, and how do we gain more control over the outcomes of our lives and the future? Are we best equipped to work individually or with others? How can we be more effective in achieving social justice goals?

Social intelligence, societies, and evolution help us to find answers to some of these basic, existential issues. For example, we know that our brains have evolved more quickly than other parts of our bodies, but at the same time we have plenty of everyday evidence that human behavior is out of control much of the time, especially in current crises. Therefore, because we need to use social intelligence to guide our actions, we reliably aspire to accomplish social justice only by implementing socially intelligent strategies.

We deal with human nature best when we face up to the difficulties we have in living up to our good intentions. For example, when we allow our emotions to take over our thinking about problematic situations, we cannot adequately consider significant aspects of social realities such as societies. We react to the immediacy of social stresses, rather than build new futures based on our thoughtful visions of improved societies.

Because of this significant human frailty, we must pay close attention to how to keep considering our situations in broad perspectives. We cannot allow individual self-centeredness to take over our assessments of our social circumstances, because our efforts to accomplish social justice would be worthless. We use our socially intelligent intentions to motivate us to stay close to our societal views of what is going on in our lives, so that we are more measured and more accurate in dealing with current social problems.

So how do we find viable ways to use societies as means to accomplish social justice goals? Our individual trial and error efforts need to be goal-directed in seeking to establish social justice, but at the same time we have to hold on to broad socially intelligent perspectives such as societies. This allows us to see which social issues we are moved by more objectively, so we persist in our efforts to use social intelligence as a means to reach social justice goals. We also assess the outcomes of our efforts, so that social facts show us the extent to which we are achieving social justice through social intelligence.

We examine our social justice practices to assess outcomes in relation to social facts. As with religious experiences, we can then draw conclusions about whether we want to live our lives with or without social intelligence and social justice. This reflection is useful because it helps us to maintain our awareness that our actions really count, and that we make significant choices in deciding how we want to direct our best efforts. Using social intelligence and societies as means to accomplish social justice actions is not a trivial matter, but rather a vital way to stay connected to effective individual and social means to accomplish our preferred goals.

Social Justice Goals

Social justice and social justice goals are needed to direct social intelligence. Only people's ethical choices, about how social intelligence increases the common good or social justice, ensure that social intelligence is useful. This is so because social intelligence can be used for either good or evil purposes. As historical actors we need to define appropriate applications of social intelligence, in order to bring about social justice goals.

Because of the power and complexities of social situations, social intelligence, and social justice, we must proceed with caution when aiming for and achieving social justice goals. Overall, we need to be true to our potentials as historical actors, so that we enter our present circumstances with informed viewpoints about the past, and clear visions of what futures could be if universal needs are met. Social intelligence requires that we approach the power and complexities of these missions through the five dimensions of social intelligence, so that we try to increase social justice in families, beliefs, social classes, cultures, and societies.

We aim to be socially intelligent in our own families, so that we gain sufficient freedom and peace of mind to envisage social justice goals in others' families and societies. Because we see that many social injustices in families occur due to uncontrolled emotions, we select options that emphasize thinking rather than emotions in our day-to-day exchanges. We also try to modify some of the hierarchical structures of family relationships, so that egalitarian family processes open up rather than close family relationships. This opening up of families' emotional systems allows families to use more authentic reciprocities, as well as experience freer expressions of emotions, thoughts, and actions.

When we try to be socially intelligent through our beliefs, we become more independent and more accurate in our thinking, assessments, and commitments. We learn how to distinguish beliefs that contradict each other, for example, from beliefs that support us in our work to make the world a better place today for tomorrow. Establishing habits of critically reviewing our beliefs helps us to clarify who we are and what we want to do with our lives, so that we go forward with socially intelligent work, such as changing social beliefs about human nature, social possibilities, and social justice.

When we use social intelligence to understand social classes more fully, we accomplish social justice goals more reliably. Immersing ourselves in social class concerns activates our social intelligence, so that we are more aware of social justice issues and solutions. For example, we may question what appeared to be a social reality—that social classes are needed for the survival of societies. Consequently social intelligence moves us, as historical actors, to change social classes by reducing their negative restrictive characteristics, so that social concerns about individual and group freedoms override motives to perpetuate social classes and social mobility within or between social classes.

Social intelligence is a means to social justice goals when we use the deep reservoirs of cultural values, ideals, expectations, and meanings to progress toward social justice. We learn how to distinguish between cultures that are constructive or destructive, life-enhancing or death-directed, and individually-oriented or collectively-oriented, so that we are more exact in our aims to establish creative and supportive cultures to improve future societies. Thus our value choices are necessary means to pursue our cultural social justice missions as historical actors.

Lastly, our societies are used as broad socially intelligent perspectives, in order to understand how historical social justice issues are achieved and implemented. For example, because of the power and complexities of globalization, we need to establish universal orientations for social justice in societies. Social intelligence helps us to understand the dynamics of maintaining and changing societies, so that we are markedly better prepared to increase national and international social justice effectively.

Our social intelligence is guided by social justice goals because this is the most practical way to create durable social justice changes. Although there is often considerable agreement that societies can meet the needs of their populations more effectively, there is much less agreement about how to accomplish this. Discussing and critically assessing alternative social justice goals helps us to create teams of like-minded workers, who are willing to serve social justice goals. Possibilities of reaching social justice goals are enhanced when we use social intelligence tools, because social intelligence principles are based on social facts.

IX. Socially Intelligent Futures and Social Justice

When we commit ourselves to using social intelligence to create socially intelligent futures, we find that these goals overlap with goals to increase social justice. Socially intelligent views and actions, in relation to existing social realities, predictably usher in improved social conditions, which make social justice more viable in the present for an ever-expanding future. Because social awareness of the power and complexities of the five major social influences of families, beliefs, social classes, cultures, and societies alone cannot guarantee social justice—constructive social attitudes do not consistently produce constructive social actions—we are beholden to the socially intelligent principles of needing to make improved value choices and to take actions that ensure social justice is accomplished.

In these respects, social intelligence—especially when it is deliberately nurtured—ultimately tends to culminate in increasing social justice. However, even in such optimal conditions, we also need social justice ideals to pull us toward accomplishing specific social justice goals, in order to be as effective and successful as possible in creating socially intelligent futures. Because social intelligence cannot produce socially intelligent futures that are synonymous with social justice, we must be inspired by additional social justice ideals in order to produce our best futures.

The critical supportive and inspirational roles that social justice plays, in guiding our socially intelligent actions, increases our odds for making individual and social changes to increase social justice. Although social intelligence may motivate us to proceed toward social justice, more importantly our individual and social value choices of social justice ideals—such as equality, inclusiveness, diversity, cooperation, and openness—direct us to attain social justice. Social justice uses social intelligence to create socially intelligent futures that strengthen social justice, by focusing on social justice ideals and optimal social conditions for social justice.

To the extent that social intelligence produces benefits for all through social justice ideals, social justice results from understanding the significance of the social facts that underlie social intelligence principles and actions. For example, social facts about families, beliefs, social classes, cultures, and societies clarify our socially intelligent goals as well as our long-term efforts to increase the common good and social justice. A fuller grasp of social realities heightens our awareness of what we need to change in order to accomplish social justice, so we can continue to use social intelligence to inform and guide us in our everyday social justice actions.

Nevertheless, even when we rely on social facts and social intelligence to guide us, we are easily overwhelmed by the substantive power and complexities of our families, beliefs, social classes, cultures, and societies. We turn to social justice to aim for higher social ideals than social intelligence, so that we can persist in our efforts to work toward our goals in spite of many tenacious difficulties. Thus, when we use social justice to inspire social intelligence, we transcend our everyday frustrations and attain our most constructive social justice goals.

Therefore, social justice ideals, not merely social intelligence principles, help us to reach our goals as historical actors who work cooperatively with likeminded others to increase the common good. For example, social intelligence allows us to see more clearly that social justice is where we want to go, and that our journeys to reach this goal can be transformed by keeping social justice ideals at the forefront of our concerns. Focusing on how we contribute to the common good and social justice helps us to see ourselves, others, and the world differently, so that we can make deeper commitments to pursue and achieve social justice.

Social intelligence continues to increase our knowledge of social influences and of who we are. Our enriched understanding turns us toward social justice, and makes choosing social justice options more viable in our daily actions and ultimate fulfillment. For example, because we are inspired by our deeper awareness of the power and complexities of the five social influences of families, beliefs, social classes, cultures, and societies, we find new opportunities to be more responsible in planning better futures. Furthermore, even though our external lives may not immediately appear to be qualitatively different, we see that moving toward social justice adds meaning to our lives, and increases the freedom of others as well as ourselves.

Social Justice as Vision of the Future

Because social justice is often not sufficiently self-evident in the present, it is essentially a utopian vision of the future. However, because social intelligence derives from understanding past and current social facts, social justice need not be an unrealistic vision of futures, but rather visions of futures based on social facts. One of the strengths of using social intelligence to attain social justice is that we are more adept at assessing the flaws and problems of present social conditions, so that we make more enlightened decisions and commitments to bring about social justice futures.

In any event, visions of social justice based on the values of equality, inclusiveness, diversity, cooperation, and openness predictably move populations toward improved social conditions in the future. When we use social intelligence to imagine what social justice could look like and be like as day-to-day social conditions, we formulate realistic visions of societies organized around fair practices and more viable social realities. Even though we have not yet experienced societies where social justice values rule, we can surmise that it is possible to learn how to organize ourselves productively and effectively to meet the needs of all members of diverse populations.

Visions of these possibilities are important because they motivate our actions as individuals and communities. For example, by changing how we see ourselves, others, and the world, we take control of our destinies and define our futures in preferred ways. We make it possible to choose and create our futures, rather than go with the flow of current social conditions, which largely continue to reinforce the status quo.

Optimal social changes occur to the extent that we choose to focus our actions on one of the major social spheres of emotionally intense interaction in our societies: families, beliefs, social classes, cultures, or societies. For example, we start to take charge of our futures when we envision possibilities that bring equality, inclusiveness, diversity, cooperation, and openness to our families, beliefs, social classes, cultures, or societies. Thus, we make commitments with others to choose new values which aim directly at developing social justice values and social justice.

When we see our families as groups that support us rather than control us, and work to reduce some unneeded dependencies in our families, we improve our families' living conditions, so that each family member becomes stronger and more able to contribute to the common good. Similarly, when we sort out which of our beliefs are the most important to us, and which help us to reach our goals more effectively, we progress toward establishing clearer social justice visions of the future through our families and beliefs.

We also act more freely to create social justice futures when we see how short our current social classes fall from attaining social justice ideals. For example, we act more decisively to narrow social class extremes in resources and opportunities, and move toward establishing more ideal socially just conditions for the future. We also use social intelligence to assess the extent to which our cultures orient us toward destructive values rather than life-enhancing values, so that we can choose our preferred social justice values to inform our visions of the future. Furthermore, when we recognize gaps between social justice values and the social realities that exist in our cultures, as well as understand which values we need to cultivate for the present and future, we become more effective in nurturing equality, inclusiveness, diversity, cooperation, and openness.

All in all, we are responsible historical actors who have options to change the course of history in significant areas of concern, such as establishing social justice values. To the extent that we use social justice ideals to create visions of better futures, these ideals are more in our control. For example, when we share constructive visions of possibilities in societies with like-minded others, these ideals will guide our decisions and commitments in the present more effectively toward improved futures.

We cannot afford to deny the critical roles our visions play in our intentions to change social conditions in societies. For example, unless we have clarity about where we want our societies to go in the future, facts of present conditions will override our dreams. Social justice will remain a fond hope, rather than a social reality, if we do not formulate and aim for what we believe our preferred social justice futures are. In this way, our deliberately chosen values—such as equality, inclusiveness, diversity, cooperation, and openness—pave ways to accomplish social justice.

Social Justice and Social Facts

Probabilities of achieving social justice increase as we incorporate significant social facts in our plans, strategies, and actions. For example, social intelligence guides us to pay particular attention to social facts that define or express the five major social influences of families, beliefs, social classes, cultures, and societies. These social facts show us how non-rational pressures prevent us from establishing social justice and other rational goals. Furthermore, we become adept at controlling such barriers to achieving our social justice goals, only by understanding the power and complexities of the same five major social influences.

Social facts related to families show us how interdependencies recur in many social settings—such as work and political systems—and detract from clear thinking and purposive action in the interests of all members of our populations. We can only approach social justice issues of equality, inclusiveness, diversity, cooperation, and openness effectively, for example, when we discern real differences between goals that serve to satisfy narrow self-interests, and goals that are universally oriented. Social facts in families help us to make these assessments, as well as guide us to keep on our often extremely difficult tracks to achieve social justice.

We also use social facts to measure to what extent we are accomplishing the social justice goals we say we want to achieve. For example, our beliefs frequently mislead us, unless we are sufficiently objective in our assessments about what we intend to do and what we actually do. Social facts either support or refute our good intentions, because they enable us to evaluate the accuracy of our approaches to social justice goals when necessary. By contrast, going with the flow of our strongest beliefs, with complete disregard for social facts, lures us to pursue unworkable goals that do not represent the universal needs that social justice aims to meet.

Similarly, the ubiquity and power of social facts, which document the existence and impacts of social classes, may temporarily over-ride our visions of social justice, because we may not examine the assumptions we make about our particular social class situations. However, we can ensure that we use our social intelligence constructively to achieve social justice, by relating the social facts of social classes to the well-being of all. For example, we cannot afford to serve only elites in rapidly changing modern societies, because these limited groups reflect capitalist forces and special interests rather than whole populations. Conversely, we need to stay alert to social class influences through their social facts, so that we limit their restrictive biases in our collective efforts to construct social justice conditions.

Additional prejudices and discrimination because of social classes are found in cultural distortions such as racial, ethnic, and gender stereotypes. Cultures wield power as value choices that underpin our decisions, actions, and priorities. For example, social facts related to knowledge, standards, and ideals in our diverse cultures show us whether we support cultures that are life-enhancing or death-directed, individually-oriented or collectively-oriented, and constructive or destructive. In order to be effective historical actors, we must make commitments to use social facts and social intelligence to select our most vital value choices to achieve social justice. Only then can we deliberately incorporate equality, inclusiveness, diversity, cooperation, and openness in whatever we decide to accomplish to increase the common good and social justice.

Because of the impacts of our constructive value choices, we can confidently aim to change societies when we use social justice to direct our social intelligence. We continue to assess and reassess our goals and actions as historical actors, who work collectively with others to meet universal needs. At the same time, social facts help us to decide which strategies we need to create social conditions of equality, inclusiveness, diversity, cooperation, and openness throughout our societies. As long as our socially intelligent know-how is based on social facts, we are guided not only toward the common good, but also to social justice.

Because the influences of social intelligence and social justice are reciprocal—for example, we are more adept at achieving social justice when we use social intelligence—we need to increase both our social intelligence and social justice. Social facts anchor our social intelligence and root our social justice goals in current and future social realities. This means that our dreams alone are not sufficient to guide our well-intentioned actions to increase social justice, and that social justice cannot be accomplished in the long term without the pragmatic inspiration of social intelligence and social facts.

Social Justice Goals and Transcendence

Social justice is an ideal in its own right, because it helps us to transcend worldly woes and increases our efforts to achieve social justice goals. We need social justice to direct our social intelligence and socially intelligent actions, so that we can persevere in our efforts to accomplish challenging social goals. Believing in the viability of social justice makes us more effective in meeting constructive goals, and believing in the ideals of social justice prevents us from losing patience during the predictable difficulties involved in sustaining our efforts to achieve our preferred objectives in the long run.

Without the aura and glory of social justice goals, we easily get bogged down in trying to do what seems right according to social intelligence. This is so because social intelligence is more limited as a social means than social justice, and social intelligence holds us too close to mundane goals, such as making individual and social changes in power relations. By contrast, when increasing social justice is a primary goal, we find more meaningful reasons to live and act. For example, we become more aware historical actors when we are directed by worthwhile social justice ideals such as equality, and when we strengthen our purposes to make the world a better place in the future as well as the present.

Personal and social crises in families turn us toward social intelligence for its problem-solving skills, and toward social justice for imagining worlds where family members live in closer accordance with the principles of equality, inclusiveness, diversity, cooperation, and openness. We try to improve conditions in our families, for example, because we recognize the limitations of emotional interdependence that underpin our most personal relationships. Furthermore, orienting our actions toward social justice helps us to transcend the pain of loss or disappointment in family relationships, so that we weather family stresses successfully and work to accomplish social justice productively.

Believing in social justice, whatever our circumstances are, has a calming effect on our everyday anxious concerns, which otherwise may easily overwhelm us. When we clear our beliefs of contradictions, conflicts, and too much dependence on others for our fulfillment, we gain more control over our living conditions. This allows us to think clearly, formulate social justice goals, and move toward specific objectives which include working with others to achieve social justice.

In addition, focusing on social justice frees us from some of the most restrictive bonds of social classes. We neutralize or negate social classes when we use social justice to transcend contrasting social facts and conflicted schisms caused by social class privileges. Such transcendence inspires us to work toward narrowing gaps between the haves and have-nots in our communities and societies. Thus social justice is not only a viable alternative to social classes, but orients our lives toward achieving broader and deeper purposes than social classes recognize.

Cultures underpin all social groups, attitudes, and actions. When we confirm our strongest interests in social justice, we can assess how our cultures guide our actions, and to what extent social justice expresses our values and value choices. We try to create more social justice conditions now, so that social justice values improve present and future social circumstances. The shock of recognizing cultural contrasts sometimes helps us to transcend the ordinary and banal through social justice, so that these new priorities ultimately overcome whatever holds us back from making social justice progress in our cultures.

Some of our most meaningful goals are created through yearning to transcend unfavorable social situations in our societies, by reaching for social improvements that meet the needs of all. Our aspirations to impact the harshness of social realities, in the lives of those who are less privileged than we are, enable us to choose practical ideals: social intelligence guides us to create social justice in our societies and the world at large.

In these respects, we use social justice to deal with problematic social conditions in our families, beliefs, social classes, cultures, and societies. We clarify the tangled webs and contradictions of mass societies, as well as increase purpose in our lives, by assuming responsibilities as aware historical actors who work with others toward increasing the common good and social justice. The transcendence, which social justice inspires, is expressed through our individual and social value choices that cultivate equality, inclusiveness, diversity, cooperation, and openness.

Social Justice Destinations

In many respects, arriving at social justice destinations seems to be impossible. However, when we consider how to incorporate social justice into our lifetime journeys, we find that we can simplify some of the steps we need to take. For example, if we realize at the outset that even though we will never fully reach the destination of social justice, or that we will fall far short of arriving at this destination, we and others benefit from proceeding as though we may eventually reach our social justice goals. For example, we work with others more effectively when we move cooperatively and decisively in this general direction.

In some respects, our social justice destinations may be usefully considered as synonymous with our legacies. For example, we get to know who we are now by examining what we have accomplished, which includes those constructive changes we have made for ourselves and others throughout our lives. Furthermore, our goals become all-important in our lifetime assessments, because if we succeed in achieving what we set out to do, we may see that we have largely been true to ourselves, our values, and our ideals.

When we are socially intelligent, we expand our objectives to include helping others as well as ourselves. We use the broad perspectives of the five major social influences—families, beliefs, social classes, cultures, and societies—to understand our social dependencies. We also take some of our efforts out of the immediacy of the present, in order to extend our effectiveness into the future, and to consider the continued survival and well being of others as well as ourselves.

The sum total of what we have accomplished, and what we intend to accomplish, strengthens our senses of meaning, purpose, and direction. Furthermore, when we add social justice ideals as destinations for our goals, social intelligence, and daily endeavors, we become more fulfilled human beings.

Although developing our legacies may or may not generate real satisfaction in the present, there is little more that we can do than make sure we aim sufficiently high to accomplish whatever we think will bring about qualitative improvements in our worlds as we know them.

In these respects, social justice not only inspires us, but shapes our hour-by-hour motivations and actions. For example, we start each day differently because social justice is an important destination. To the extent that we deliberately focus on our families, beliefs, social classes, cultures, and societies, we proceed steadily toward social justice, by making individual and social changes that modify restrictive aspects of these major social influences.

Because we experience social justice as an eternal value, we are forever linked to its many different possibilities. For example, we may set ourselves lifetime tasks and commitments, such as strengthening the social values that make social justice possible in society at large. Consequently, we work hard to make consistent value choices of equality, inclusiveness, diversity, cooperation, and openness, so that we actively encourage improved social conditions for all. Furthermore, the universalism of our orientations for achieving social justice goals identifies us as historical actors, who are seeking to increase the common good and social justice in societies.

Because social justice orientations to actions predispose us to act in particular ways, we aim our aspirations toward worthwhile, sometimes impossible achievements related to social justice. For example, if we make personal commitments to pursue social justice for the remainder of our lifetimes, we do more to create social justice than if we did not have these goals. Even though we may not achieve what we aim for, we accomplish more than we would have otherwise.

Given the broad perspectives of social intelligence, which increase the likelihood that we will reach our destinations of social justice, we can rest assured that we have done whatever we can to accomplish social justice through our daily actions. However, we also need to deliberately renew and maintain our understanding of social justice, in order to deepen our commitments to social justice. The differences that social justice brings to our lives and actions are considerable, but we need to re-remind ourselves to focus on making socially intelligent value choices to develop immediate social conditions of equality, inclusiveness, diversity, cooperation, and openness, so that we strengthen social justice for all.

Social Justice Journeys

We may not be able to start our journeys to increase social justice at the same time that we discover social intelligence and the benefits we gain from being socially intelligent in our thoughts and actions. This is so because many people do not discover social intelligence through their efforts to achieve social justice, but rather as a consequence of needing to understand the power and complexities of social influences more fully, so that they can deal with the most troubling social issues in their everyday lives more effectively.

However, even if we may have been trying to increase social justice for a lifetime, a particular critical social situation may shock us into becoming more socially intelligent in tackling social justice issues. For example, social justice concerns related to one or more of the five major social influences of families, beliefs, social classes, cultures, and societies may jolt us into realizing how much we need to deepen our understanding of existing social issues before we can achieve success in social justice endeavors.

Whatever situations we are in, social intelligence continues to be a foundation for social justice. Unless we have a reasonably sound working knowledge of the power and complexities of families, beliefs, social classes, cultures, and societies, we cannot be significant change agents in accomplishing social justice. For example, we must be realistic in our aims to increase social justice, in order to nurture goals for collaborative work. We also consistently improve our intentions, aims, and accomplishments in social justice when we make them socially intelligent in substance and effects.

We need social intelligence to move us toward social justice goals in the earliest stages of our journeys, as well as in later stages. In fact, we may not be inspired to orient our actions toward social justice unless we already have solid foundations of social intelligence. For example, some of us need to have used socially intelligent skills before we realize that one of our best purposes may be to express our social intelligence as social justice to improve our shared futures.

So how should we proceed day by day when we want to make progress in our social justice journeys? What differences does it make to be on social justice journeys? What are the roles of social justice commitments and social justice ideals in our journeying, especially when we do not seem to be making much progress? How can we be sure that we are doing all we can to increase social justice? Whom do we need to consider before we make progress on our social justice journeys? Does everything inevitably turn out well when we are guided by social justice ideals?

We cannot be so preoccupied with social justice goals that we constantly strive for abstract goals. We have varied substantive responsibilities that need to be met, and being over-responsible may be little more than an over-reaction. We need to learn how to balance our efforts to meet family members' real needs with how we pursue social justice ideals that transcend our daily business.

Thus, sorting out our priorities is necessary before we can develop work patterns that are conducive to collaborating with others to achieve social justice goals. We do not leave our responsibilities behind when we pursue lofty ideals, but rather learn to establish calm working conditions, so that we can pursue social justice goals. When we are sufficiently socially intelligent to meet our responsibilities, and know what we want to accomplish with our lives, we are perhaps ready to journey more directly toward social justice goals.

When we use social justice ideals to map out destinations for our socially intelligent journeys, we are well-prepared to deal with whatever comes our way during these journeys. For example, we hone our skills in social intelligence, so that the allures of families, beliefs, social classes, cultures, and societies do not get the better of us and drain our energies through multiple diversions or conflicts. Rather, we bring the power and complexities of the five major social influences of families, beliefs, social classes, cultures, and societies more directly under our control by resisting their pressures, rather than by going along with their pressures to conform to conventional standards that uphold the status quo.

Making value choices to increase equality, inclusiveness, diversity, cooperation, and openness on a daily basis characterizes our social justice journeys. Even though we may orient our thinking toward social justice ideals at the outset of each day, we still need to establish new value choices of equality, inclusiveness, diversity, cooperation, and openness in whatever we do with others to achieve social justice and live fully.

Social Justice and Social Intelligence

At best social intelligence shows us different ways to achieve social justice. Although social intelligence can be used for good or evil purposes, *Social Intelligence and Social Justice* demonstrates how social intelligence enhances individual and social efforts to achieve social justice, and how social justice adds meanings and purposes to social intelligence. Even though social justice is an ideal which may transcend all other goals, the emphasis here is that we must ultimately pay attention to understanding the social conditions we are dealing with, in order to accomplish social justice.

Thus, we can surmise that social justice, as both a social ideal and a social reality, depends on being socially intelligent about dealing with hazardous and routine social conditions that restrict rather than free individuals and groups of people to achieve their most cherished goals. Although social intelligence is not an end in itself—we do not strive merely to increase our social intelligence—we need to continue to increase our social intelligence in order to be fully alert to the power and complexities of major social influences, as well as to use our potentials as much as possible to achieve worthwhile social justice goals.

Social justice is complex, so that unless social justice incorporates social intelligence, social justice may be too difficult to maintain and will not last. Social intelligence is necessary to social justice, because without it we may merely be fooling ourselves that we know what social justice is when we do not. We deliberately cultivate and express social intelligence in order to create socially just societies, which are firmly rooted in social justice values such as equality, inclusiveness, diversity, cooperation, and openness.

We understand the emotional pull of major social influences in societies when we see how love is easily mistaken or misguided in patterns of family interaction and personal relations. Even though love is unchallenged as a mainstay of modern families, much mischief is done in the name of love—as in the name of religion—which actually limits and restricts individuals and groups rather than frees them to be themselves.

We cannot claim to understand and be directed by social justice if this is an empty call which merely covers up problematic social issues, attitudes, and behaviors. We use social intelligence to keep us honest about our families, beliefs, social classes, cultures, and societies so that we do not assert only our vested interests, or endeavor to meet only our personal wants, rather than seek to meet universal needs. Gaining more control over our reactions to families, beliefs, social classes, cultures, and societies makes us stronger in our commitments and actions, so that we are effective socially intelligent historical actors who increase social justice.

Because it is necessary to first recognize our social situations for what they are, it is only after we are aware of social intelligence, and the differences that social intelligence makes in our lives, that we can apply our socially intelligent skills fully to increasing the common good and social justice. However, social intelligence is not merely a preamble for attaining social justice, but rather a continuing guide to shed light on what social justice is, and how we can attain social justice alone or with others. Although we use social justice to deal with the complex and powerful influences of families, beliefs, social classes, cultures, and societies, whatever we aspire to also needs to be viewed from broad social intelligence perspectives.

We need to understand the relentlessness of social issues related to families, beliefs, social classes, cultures, and societies, and to feel the pull and push of their social pressures to conform and accept the status quo. Both social intelligence and social justice show us important changes to reorganize our societies, and we must at the same time use social intelligence to understand the implications, causes, and consequences of social justice. This helps us to establish social conditions in families, beliefs, social classes, cultures, and societies that encourage individual and social value choices such as equality, inclusiveness, diversity, cooperation, and openness.

Although social justice directs social intelligence in distinctive ways, social justice does not replace social intelligence. Social intelligence principles are vital means to be objective, to be critical, to understand different time perspectives, and to be discerning historical actors. Social justice is strengthened when social intelligence is expressed individually and socially, because it needs foundations of social facts in order to endure. Furthermore, unless we are socially intelligent, we may not be able to make commitments to address social justice issues effectively.

Social Intelligence
Creates Social Justice

X. Social Realities and Social Justice

Even though social justice is a social ideal, we cannot hope to achieve social justice by thinking only at abstract levels of understanding. We need to establish our intentions through actions, such as by acting with like-minded people who want to achieve social justice. For example, we try to deal directly and collectively with social facts that describe and explain our current situations, especially when the social realities expressed in these social facts are either harsh or unwanted. In fact, we only progress toward our ideals of social justice when we compare and contrast current social realities with idealistic social justice goals. Thus the business that we are about is to close gaps between our ideals of social justice and existing social realities that create restrictive social conditions in our everyday lives.

Social intelligence helps us to accomplish practical social justice tasks efficiently and effectively. We use social intelligence to understand the main characteristics of our current social realities, and to recognize how we can achieve social justice through socially intelligent actions. Social intelligence is a means both to achieve specific social justice goals, and to guide us toward increasing social justice in diverse situations. Consequently, we become highly motivated agents of social change, as well as effective historical actors who are committed to increasing social justice.

Because of the key roles played by social realities and social intelligence in these social processes, we understand how social intelligence can be thought of as creating social justice. By inspiring corrective actions suggested by social realities, social intelligence uses social facts to increase opportunities for all, whatever social sphere we work in with others to meet our shared social justice goals. We study significant social facts, because they help us to define social realities in our current situations, and we find ways out of conflicting social issues by using social intelligence and social justice to guide our actions and commitments.

For example, the broad perspectives of social intelligence help us to focus on the social realities of our families. We see that some of the repetitions in our families' behaviors, especially between members of different generations, perpetuate problems in dealing with families' present situations, as well as in long-term plans to launch families' youngest members into societies and the world. Furthermore, it is often only by paying close attention to immediate needs in families' interdependence, that we can see what we must do to increase independence within and among families.

Different social realities help us to understand the power and complexities of our beliefs. Whether or not we are religious, clusters of beliefs may restrict our most well-intentioned actions, so that we ignore some of the social realities that underlie undesirable social conditions in our everyday lives. Social intelligence helps us to assess the extent to which our current beliefs hold us back from achieving social justice goals, and patterns in social realities suggest new directions for using social intelligence principles to achieve social justice. We educate our beliefs through facing the facts of our social situations, which increases probabilities that we will achieve social justice successfully.

In addition, social intelligence may begin to create social justice when we seriously consider the extent to which social classes dominate our thoughts and actions. For example, we become more in charge of our thinking about present social realities when we examine social facts and social realities in our past and present social class allegiances. However, in spite of insisting that we want to make social classes more equal, we are often caught up in self-interests or social class interests, that repeat past behaviors and uphold existing social class inequalities.

Cultures are another strong omnipresent influence on how we connect current social realities with social justice ideals. Social intelligence helps us to achieve social justice when we acknowledge the omnipresence of cultures and their impacts on specific qualities of our lives. In addition, acknowledging the power and complexities of cultures enables us not to give up on significant aspects of social justice, before we reach our social justice goals. Social intelligence teaches us to see our cultures for what they are, as well as to respect the power of cultural social realities, as we proceed toward social justice.

Lastly, social intelligence is applied directly to social justice concerns when we assess the strengths and weaknesses of our societies. Societies enable us to consider some of the broadest concerns of social justice, which helps us to meet universal needs rather than special interest needs in our populations. Because social realities are repeated patterns of behavior through time, we broaden our perspectives by assessing the extent to which we organize our day-to-day lives around being historical actors in our societies.

The following subsections of this chapter of *Social Intelligence and Social Justice* trace how some of the influences of social realities in families, beliefs, social classes, cultures, and societies make significant differences to accomplishing social justice. They also highlight how these five major social influences work in social intelligence, and how social intelligence creates social justice.

Social Realities and Families

Social intelligence is a necessary condition, but not a sufficient condition, for achieving social justice. Although we may choose to constantly strive for the ideals of social justice as social ideals, the odds of our achieving social justice are much lower when we stay in realms of abstractions, than when we focus on dealing with the social facts and social realities of our given situations in socially intelligent ways. In these respects it is much to our benefit, and to the benefit of others, when we focus on being socially intelligent in achieving social justice.

Although perhaps few people would agree that social intelligence creates social justice, in the best case scenarios this is possible, and in the usual circumstances of everyday lives, social justice is more likely to develop from using socially intelligent strategies. Because social intelligence is such a vital cornerstone in our enlightened efforts to increase social justice, we benefit from remembering that families are an exceptionally strong social influence in nurturing our capacities to be socially intelligent. For example, it is important to understand patterns of dependencies in our families, because these reflect the deepest parts of our positive and negative emotions. In fact, unless we learn how to handle strong non-rational influences in our own lives, we will be less astute in achieving social justice.

The social facts and social realities we need to recognize and deal with require us to be objective about the emotional systems of families, which may otherwise dominate our lives. For example, when we understand the extent to which our families are open or closed social systems, which support or burden us because of how they function in their everyday exchanges, we try to settle family issues that need attention before we assume responsibilities as historical actors who work to increase social justice. We assess different constructive contributions we could make in our families that would not burden other family members. We also identify how we can be freer in our socially intelligent choices to increase the common good and social justice.

Because we acknowledge the compelling power of families when we commit ourselves to increasing social intelligence, we understand social facts and social realities more realistically. For example, we see more clearly how families influence our beliefs, social classes, cultures, and societies, and how our emotional orientations to ourselves, others, and the world result from what has occurred in past and present patterns of family interactions. Qualities in our ongoing social networks derive from whether or not we relate independently with significant others in our families and varied social settings.

An interesting starting point for observing how we deal with our families, communities, and the world is to consider families' histories from the viewpoints of particular sibling positions. We then understand more fully some of the intergenerational pressures we experienced, and which values were used through the generations to inspire or control family members. For example, we see that if we are oldest children or only children, we may be family favorites of parents and grandparents, and that this intense focus in our families' emotional systems is not as productive for achieving freedom and social justice as other sibling positions which are less special or less coveted.

Our historical roles in families, as well as the trajectories of our parents, show us how families make everyday distinctions between the past, present, and future that we too may have used automatically. Because families are important sources of basic attitudes, such as views about time, we see how often we are subjected to relatives' ways of valuing time, unless we deliberately cultivate attitudes of being critical about the many complex ways our families impact us.

Qualitative family influences remind us of our priorities to become more socially intelligent, by suggesting social facts and social realities that influence how we act. Our struggles to become more objective about family influences, which include assessing repeated patterns of interaction through time, prepare us for the many challenges of trying to be socially intelligent in increasing social justice. Consequently, we appreciate the social reality that it is only when our family pressures are manageable that we function sufficiently well to pursue social justice productively. Both understanding our families and increasing our social intelligence make us more aware of social justice possibilities.

Social Realities and Beliefs

Relationships between social realities and beliefs, as well as between social realities and families, show us that social intelligence is critical for increasing social justice. For example, to the extent that beliefs are substantiated by social facts and social realities, beliefs can be a moving force which supports both social intelligence and social justice. However, when beliefs are unrealistic, dogmatic, distortions of social realities, or confused, they cannot motivate or guide socially intelligent actions to accomplish social justice. Even though we often define beliefs conventionally as expressing faith in the unseen, or as manifesting our own unique interpretations of social reality, we need to be sufficiently rooted in shared beliefs that reflect significant social realties, in order to be effective historical actors.

Shared beliefs undergird all four of the other major social influences that are at the core of our social intelligence: families, social classes, cultures, and societies. This means that what we think or feel is true is not only a strong motivating factor in making decisions, making commitments, increasing social intelligence, and achieving social justice, but belief in truth is itself a social reality and a major social influence in its own right. However, because there is usually a critical gap between what we believe and what is real, we need to adapt and accommodate our beliefs in strategic ways that directly reflect our social justice goals and intentions, as well as our achievements.

When we deliberately create optimistic beliefs, in order to increase our motivation for achieving social justice goals, we control the extent to which we envision hopeful conditions and outcomes through our persistent efforts. However, if our beliefs essentially deny social realities, we find that we are not sufficiently objective or mature to deal with existing conditions realistically, so we fall short of reaching our social justice goals satisfactorily. Furthermore, we may delude ourselves into thinking that our denials of reality are more valuable guides for our decisions and behavior than either social intelligence or social justice.

In the same ways that we deliberately examine families and their influences on our behavior, particularly on non-rational or emotional behavior, we also need to scrutinize our beliefs and the content of our beliefs, in order to understand whether or not our beliefs support us in our endeavors to reach socially intelligent goals and social justice. For example, we examine the most basic of our strongest beliefs, as well as the assumptions we make about families, religions, sciences, social classes, cultures, and societies. When we review the beliefs of particular religions or sciences, however, we may see that clusters of their beliefs and values frequently guide us in particular directions without our realizing it, or without our wanting this to be so.

A close assessment of our beliefs and their impacts on our lives sharpens our awareness of the extent to which we accept our beliefs as social realities. For example, we need to consider the extent to which we remain open to learning new social facts, so that we change our beliefs effectively when necessary. Social intelligence encourages us to continuously face social facts and social realities, so that we do not hide from the world and our responsibilities through using limited or opaque beliefs. Ultimately, we benefit most from staying open to many possibilities to refine and consolidate our beliefs. This means that we serve ourselves and others best through amassing beliefs which directly express both social realities and social justice goals.

When we succeed in aligning our beliefs with our understanding of ourselves, others, and the world, we become more effective historical actors who increase social justice. We use social intelligence to reach social justice goals, because social justice goals are constructive responses to the social realities and social facts of our given situations. Social intelligence helps us to create social justice, and new social realities come into being. Furthermore, we continue to ensure social justice in the future by creating social conditions that support new values such as equality, inclusiveness, diversity, cooperation, and openness.

When we take steps to use social intelligence to create social justice, we reduce the likelihood that our beliefs will blind us, tie us into unwise commitments, or raise false hopes. The social facts and social realities of our particular situations keep us focused on beliefs about what exists, which enables us to develop social justice goals to improve current social conditions. Consequently, being responsible historical actors strengthens life-enhancing beliefs, which construct more promising futures for all.

Social Realities and Social Classes

In many instances, social justice is intimately involved with complex issues about social classes. For example, the five values of equality, inclusiveness, diversity, cooperation, and openness used in *Social Intelligence and Social Justice,* illustrate value choices that are conducive to establishing social justice conditions, and that at the same time challenge well-established assumptions about social classes. Equality, inclusiveness, diversity, cooperation, and openness describe and explain power relations that predictably break down some of the most relentless hierarchies and inequalities of social classes.

When we first become aware of social intelligence, it is perhaps easiest to relate our experiences and observations of societies to the injustices involved in social classes. However, social classes and social justice may also be considered in the contexts of our families, beliefs, cultures, history, and globalization. For example, as children we may have been mystified about why and how social class differences existed, as well as why and how social class differences are perpetuated without much widespread concern or discussion. Social intelligence frequently evokes some of our earlier expressions of shock and resolve to change social classes, because we now take a closer look at the social facts of our situations, and the social realities of the social classes which permeate all known societies and restrict social opportunities for the good life.

When we are sufficiently socially intelligent to realize that we want to commit ourselves to achieving social justice as best we can, we understand more of the power and complexities of the social forces that create and perpetuate social classes. For example, the task of modifying social classes, so they are advantageous to all members of populations, appears to be monumental or impossible. However, social intelligence teaches us that increasing our social intelligence is the most effective step to take to create social justice, especially by working cooperatively and openly with others.

Increasing our social intelligence helps us to accept our individual and social realities in becoming more responsible historical actors. We may then choose to assess characteristics of social classes, as well as start socially intelligent projects that narrow restrictive contrasts between and among different social classes. For example, we increasingly recognize that social classes are both traditional and modern in contemporary societies, and that we need to examine social facts about social classes based on religion, education, race, ethnicity, gender, sexual orientation, ablebodiedness, social connections, and social status, as well as about social classes based on economic resources.

Our recognition of the complexities involved in defining social classes moves us in productive directions to consider social facts that impinge on the lives of all people in all societies. Because it is increasingly apparent that societies throughout the world are grouped according to power and prestige, the opportunities available to members of particular societies now depend on international as well as national hierarchies. Thus, although we are all global citizens, we at the same time participate fully in our own societies' social classes based on current national boundaries.

In light of these critical categories of national and international social classes, our work to increase social justice—both within and outside societal boundaries—needs to account for the many complex nuances in social class differences. For example, whereas some contemporary societies have traditional social classes dominated by local customs, other contemporary societies have social classes primarily characterized by modern cultural styles, with fewer social classes based on economic resources. Consequently, the resistance that populations muster, when attempts are made to apply social justice to social classes, or to create alternatives to social classes, is only effectively overcome when we use social intelligence to guide us.

Social justice work is not complete if it does not create more equality, inclusiveness, diversity, cooperation, and openness. In order to accomplish these improved social conditions, however, we need to make effective changes in existing social classes. For example, because social classes are found in all societies in all times and all places, our social justice efforts must include dealing with social class inequalities, if we are to create socially intelligent futures and social justice. These goals necessitate working cooperatively with others, as well as designing non-hierarchical ways of organizing our communities and societies. Furthermore, the importance of being guided by social intelligence in all these endeavors, suggests the extent to which social intelligence creates social justice.

Social Realities and Cultures

Although it may appear to people who work toward increasing social justice that social intelligence, social facts, social realities, and cultures have little or no influence on the attainment of social justice, this is inaccurate. For example, social intelligence shows us that we need to know significant social facts about our present circumstances before we can be truly effective in reaching any intended goals of increasing social justice. This means that the risks and hazards involved in aiming blindly toward unclear goals of social justice are necessarily self-defeating and unproductive, especially when compared to more enlightened agendas of allowing social intelligence to guide social justice work.

However, if we are already convinced that it is advisable to take into account the influences of social realities in our current situations, we must still ask why we need to understand how cultures are particularly significant social influences that either hinder or support individual and collective efforts to achieve social justice. When we examine cultures as one of the five major social influences that govern our understanding of social intelligence principles, we see that cultures are primary sources of our value choices, and that we must turn to cultures to understand the substance of our motives, goals, and achievements.

Cultures are more than the context or content of our goals, because they are at the heart of our being and acting. For example, cultures make up our highest aims and best intentions. In some respects we are our cultures because our identities derive from our preferred cultural values and our preferred cultural choices. For example, social intelligence teaches us that when we are socially intelligent responsible historical actors, we achieve social justice both directly and indirectly by changing our necessary value choices to include emphases on values such as equality, inclusiveness, diversity, cooperation, and openness. These value choices bring about gradual social changes that ultimately transform our social conditions, so that they support rather than reduce or destroy social justice.

Our overall efforts to achieve social justice require us to relate differently to the five major social influences of families, beliefs, social classes, cultures, and societies. For example, when we realize the power and complexities of these five major social influences, we understand more fully how the emotional content of these social forces may derail our best intentions and plans. Unless we prepare ourselves by strengthening our social intelligence, we easily spin our wheels unproductively in misguided efforts to accomplish social justice, or become overwhelmed by the non-rational social influences we necessarily encounter in pursuing social justice goals.

Social justice values guide our cultural choices, so that our daily value choices give us reasons to live fully through keeping others' needs in focus as well as our own. To the extent that social justice is defined as responding to the universal needs of populations, we proceed strong in the knowledge that we are doing whatever we can now for the present and future needs of those who are less advantaged. However, our social justice orientations need to be truly pluralistic in terms of their foundation values of equality, inclusiveness, diversity, cooperation, and openness if we are to be effective in addressing significant social justice issues on a continuing basis.

Repetitions in value choices are some of the most significant social realities in our cultures. For example, because cultural values frequently take on lives of their own, social intelligence shows us that the social justice values emphasized in *Social Intelligence and Social Justice* are not necessarily new values, but rather values that were periodically endorsed for particular purposes through the ages, often in isolation from each other rather than clustered together. The new awareness that social intelligence brings to bear on societies and social conditions that need to be opened up by social justice values, is that individual and collective goals of constructive social change can be accomplished by transforming social justice values such as equality, inclusiveness, diversity, cooperation, and openness into social realities.

The pervasiveness of social realities in cultures, and values in cultures, requires us to be socially intelligent at every move. This is not that we use relentless, humorless disciplines in our social justice work, but rather that we are creative in different endeavors to usher in less popular cultural values. For example, in some hedonistic cultures of present-day wealthy modern societies, it seems unthinkable for privileged individuals and groups to focus on their responsibilities for whole societies and the qualities of globalization. By contrast, social intelligence gives us broad perspectives that invite challenges to improve social conditions. Whereas we might not have previously thought that we needed the guidance of social intelligence, we gain immediate dividends from increased meaningfulness by using social intelligence principles to make new value choices, which create more just worlds.

Social Realities and Societies

Repeated patterns of interaction in societies, which make up some of our most significant social realities, are often the most difficult aspects of our social environments to change. For example, traditions and social institutions, such as legal systems and governments, may have stayed in place for centuries. However, although we are undoubtedly subjected to historical forces, which are usually experienced as external objective influences, social intelligence shows us that we can control significant aspects of social realities in societies.

Social intelligence is particularly useful in helping us to see and assess the power and complexities of the broadest social realities of families, beliefs, social classes, cultures, and societies. Social intelligence reminds us that some of the most vital consequences of being historical actors are that we realize that what we do about historical trends is largely up to us, and that historical trends do not determine our destinies. Therefore, we may choose to deliberately change established patterns of interactions collectively, or accept the status quo by continuing to reinforce existing social injustices.

One of the many different ways, in which members of societies have opportunities to control their destinies in the present and future, is to formulate social policies to meet the universal needs of members of their populations. Even though radical social changes cannot be brought into being quickly through new laws, being responsible leaders of efforts that enlighten ways to increase societies' access to resources, eventually benefits societies as well as their individual members. For example, we enrich our societies when we increase access to social opportunities and social advantages, rather than merely diminish existing social privileges. Thus, our socially intelligent goals can be thought of as how to distribute upper class privileges to all, by meeting the real needs for each person to be both constructive and productive.

Social policies, that improve education at elementary and secondary levels for children with inadequate social resources, ultimately benefit all members of societies rather than just some children. Also, if historical actors use social intelligence to devise ways to improve opportunities for all children, social justice needs may be met in the short and long run. Moreover, even when this work is largely unfinished, heading in such life-enhancing directions ensures that we continue to increase the common good and social justice in varied ways.

If those who want to implement constructive changes in education or other social spheres are resisted, organizing like-minded people who want universal improvements throughout societies, adds the support necessary for incorporating new ideas and innovative methods. Eventually, these grass roots strategies may result in legislative changes. For example, social movements that address needs for improved education may attract additional resources for this purpose, or may facilitate the transfer of already-existing public funds for these endeavors. Even though these challenging social processes often turn out to be lengthy efforts, especially when public resistance is strong, taking collective action in significant areas of concern is crucial for accomplishing social justice.

Thus social intelligence gives us reliable broad views that shed light on the pros and cons of working on controversial issues that increase social justice. We benefit from meeting these ideas head on, and through confronting social realities directly. This enables us to use our know-how about the five major influences of families, beliefs, social classes, cultures, and societies wisely, especially by identifying emotional hot spots of resistance to our socially intelligent, social justice plans. For example, when we understand the destructive power of ignorance, bigotry, and denial, we do better to persist in our responsible efforts to achieve social justice, than to turn away from these difficult challenges.

We may work hard to accomplish social justice in our families, beliefs, social classes, and cultures, but it will not be until we are aware of those societal trends which hamper our efforts to increase social justice the most, that we see the true broader picture of our successes and failures. Furthermore, it is imperative that we keep broad socially intelligent perspectives clearly in mind, at the same time that we proceed to apply principles of social intelligence to social justice in our personal lives, families, communities, societies, and the international community. Such a stretched vision helps us to build social justice futures, as well as brings social justice to bear on present social realities.

Social Realities, Social Intelligence, and Social Justice

Unless social realities are recognized and dealt with through social intelligence, they may hold back even our best-intentioned efforts to increase social justice. Because social realities are usually taken for granted, or are thought to be unchangeable social facts, they often remain unquestioned in their power and complexities, being treated as though they have eternal claims to their existence and current characteristics. However, because social intelligence both urges and teaches us to cultivate effective questioning attitudes about social realities, we sometimes err on the side of questioning social realities too much rather than insufficiently.

In any event, social realities continue to exist in one form or another, and in one set of social practices or another. We are societies because people have continuities in their patterned exchanges and reciprocities. Nevertheless, responsible and free historical actors, who deliberately apply social intelligence principles, can choose to create alternatives to existing social realities, as well as new social processes and new futures. For example, making value choices that express equality, inclusiveness, diversity, cooperation, and openness, enables us to establish social conditions that support social justice, as well as modes of creativity that inspire, motivate, and achieve social justice conditions for universal needs.

In these respects, we should not passively fear the power and complexities of social realities, nor feel helpless in light of the power and complexities of social realities. As long as we do our best to stay awake to choices and change possibilities related to social justice, we can actively usher in improved futures in response to the impacts of destructive social realities in our problematic pasts and the present. However, we cannot take life-enhancing changes for granted, because many complex critical choices and changes are involved in creating better futures.

Examining social realities in our families, beliefs, social classes, cultures, and societies shows us directions for our initial collaborative efforts to achieve social justice. Consequently, we become familiar with nuances in the social realities of the five major social influences of families, beliefs, social classes, cultures, and societies, as well as with possibilities for expressing the social justice value choices of equality, inclusiveness, diversity, cooperation, and openness. We also focus on individual and collaborative efforts that modify our relationships and actions in relation to existing and new social realities, so that we become more responsible present-oriented and future-oriented historical actors.

We acknowledge the power of families as emotional systems within our families and societies, so that we gain some control over the non-rational components of our existing social realities. This allows us to think more clearly about which social realities we want to construct for better futures, and we become more independent as adult children, spouses, and parents who pass on this invaluable independence to our children and members of our youngest generations. In these ways, new repeated social realities in families support their members more strongly, so that universal needs are better met in the present for the future.

When we recognize the emotional, non-rational aspects of our individual and social beliefs, we gain clarity in assessing which of our beliefs support or diminish social justice values and processes. For example, in building new societies, we want our beliefs to be well-coordinated among themselves and in relation to others' beliefs. Although social justice is a beacon which combines individual and social efforts to create new social realities that support the well-being of whole societies, we still need to act decisively and make clear commitments to socially intelligent, social justice goals in order to achieve them.

We use social intelligence to connect the social realities of social classes, cultures, and societies to social justice. This means that social intelligence is a significant pivot or catalyst in our attempts to honor existing social realities and social justice ideals. For example, social intelligence helps us to bring social justice goals to life, so that we eventually share the enlightenment of social justice. These new everyday assumptions and values guide our behavior, and make us more aware of the choices we have and the changes we can make in favor of social justice.

XI. Socially Intelligent Choices and Social Justice

In many respects making socially intelligent choices ensures the attainment of social justice in the long run. Social intelligence creates social justice by bringing about specific social conditions. For example, choices and decisions which reflect principles of knowledge about the five major social influences of families, beliefs, social classes, cultures, and societies guide us to create circumstances that support social justice values such as equality, inclusiveness, diversity, cooperation, and openness. Thus, to the extent that we become what we do, our actions as responsible historical actors make social justice possible.

The centrality of social intelligence in this sequence of events and accomplishments results from continuing to pay close attention to the choices we make in relation to families, beliefs, social classes, cultures, and societies. Securing socially intelligent contacts and exchanges with these five major social influences inspires, motivates, and ensures that we are more inclined to choose social justice values such as equality, inclusiveness, diversity, cooperation, and openness in whatever we do. Consequently, our present and future actions are more effective in accomplishing and maintaining social justice, even though social intelligence is a necessary rather than a sufficient contribution toward accomplishing social justice. Ideally, our actions extend our everyday uses of social intelligence, so that they encompass specific social justice goals as needed.

When we examine the choices we make in relation to families, social intelligence helps us to assess the extent to which we meet the real needs of our family members, as well as the universal real needs of others' family members, especially in relation to whether people can live full and productive lives. Socially intelligent principles encourage family exchanges that give freedom and independence to family members whenever possible, although in the short run shared existential needs of subsistence and basic services should be met as high priorities. This is a tall order, but social intelligence views families as starting points or foundations that strengthen social intelligence, and as effective launching pads to increase the common good and social justice in society and the world.

The choices we make in relation to our beliefs also need to be scrutinized. Beliefs are particularly significant for pursuing social justice goals, because beliefs often determine the power of our motivations and commitments that aim our actions toward attaining social justice ideals. For example, we need to strengthen our faith in possibilities and the unseen forces we encounter in our everyday lives, as well as in the tangible goals we think of as socially intelligent social justice objectives. It is difficult to be realistic in maintaining this balance, but we build more solid beliefs and social justice pursuits when we let go of beliefs that predictably lead us in unproductive, destructive, or even lethal directions. We replace contradictory beliefs, and strengthen practical social justice beliefs, when we choose to consciously cultivate beliefs that are productive, constructive, and life enhancing in relation to the broad perspectives of social intelligence.

When we make socially intelligent choices for social justice, we also opt not to support, reinforce, or repeat social class behaviors that recreate past and present social realities of social classes. In fact, to the extent that we aim for socially intelligent or social justice ideals, we benefit from deliberately trying to find or develop non-hierarchical ways to organize ourselves and our communities, because this strengthens cooperative and open ways of interacting. Even if we cannot find or create viable alternatives to social classes, we can choose to persist in narrowing the ever-widening gaps in resources and opportunities that hold in place the marked differences between the life chances of wealthy and poor people in both traditional and modern contemporary societies.

In addition, we choose to let social intelligence guide us toward social justice by changing our cultures and societies. Although we may ultimately strive to bring about social justice changes, we start and continue this progress by scrutinizing our choices in relation to cultures and societies, at each stage of our journeys as responsible historical actors. For example, we choose to focus on changing our cultural values, so that we are more active and more selective in determining which constructive values need to be more robust in our societies. By encouraging social justice value choices in the present, and making choices to perpetuate social justice values in the future, we use social intelligence to create social justice. Thus, we invest in futures that create social justice for all.

Socially Intelligent Choices and Families

Social intelligence emphasizes the importance of cultivating our capacities to be objective about self, life, others, and the world. For example, taking a step back in our daily lives allows us many more options to make choices about how we think and what we do, than if we stay rooted in the midst of the emotional hurly burly of our reactive conventional exchanges. Above all, we need to become more objective about our own families and families in general, if we are to be as resourceful as possible in our given situations.

When we manage to be more objective and more critical, we gain control over our reactions to some of our family pressures. This is particularly important because if we do not know how to say no to relatives' pressures to conform to family expectations, or to doing things the same as other family members over several generations, we are not sufficiently free to choose critical aspects of our lives. By contrast, when we take socially intelligent steps to be more independent in our exchanges with family members, we recognize options that we missed before. Thus, our attempts to use social intelligence to guide our family choices make significant differences to the outcomes of our social justice work.

Social intelligence teaches us to respect the power and complexities of our families by examining the extent to which our families control our energies. For example, when we are comfortably ensconced in our families, especially in terms of their expectations for us, we may not at the same time understand the importance of striving to be objective about our choices and decisions. Social intelligence guides us to pay attention to how we benefit from balancing our family obligations with our strategies to live fully, so that we do not repeat unproductive modes of being, spin our wheels, or dissipate our creative energies.

Sometime it is difficult to see our families for what they are, in order to assess both near and distant family interactions objectively. Knowing families as emotional systems of interdependence helps us to realize what we need to do to be open and cooperative in our families, so that each family member thrives and prospers. We need to give others the freedoms we want and need, so that we allow them to become independent through the best conditions possible.

Applying social justice ideals to our families may not always be feasible, partly because it is very difficult to be objective about what social justice means in personal terms, or about how we think we can work cooperatively with other members of our families to meet social justice goals. However, to the extent that social intelligence heightens our awareness of the social fact that we are all historical actors, we can see that we need to apply our socially intelligent know-how to meeting universal family needs. For example, social intelligence helps us to realize the foundational importance of our family choices, so we are more inspired to spread these advantages to others and their families. This allows us to begin to resolve more widespread social intelligence and social justice issues.

When we focus on trying to understand the emotional significance of family exchanges, we necessarily expand our interests in social intelligence and social justice. Even if we cannot arrive at what we consider to be the achievement of social intelligence and social justice in our own families, we can join with others who are committed to making viable family conditions more possible in our stressful lives. Finding alternative ways to accomplish family business, for example, may relieve other families if not our own, which makes it sufficiently worth our while to continue to develop our social intelligence and social justice skills.

When we persist in focusing on the significance of our families, and the critical importance of social intelligence in making family choices, we increase social justice. Our good intentions come to fruition because we proceed carefully, and at the same time deliberately cultivate skills in being objective. For example, we critically assess how we and our family members often deny or avoid responsibilities, so that we can proceed with confidence that we are on the right track to discovering who we really are, and what we want to accomplish in terms of social justice in our families and others' families.

Socially Intelligent Choices and Beliefs

In the same way that we respect the significance of the impacts of our family beliefs on our actions and social intelligence, we need to become more familiar with the extent to which all of our most deep-seated beliefs help or hinder us to increase our social intelligence, make decisions, and pursue social justice. This level of awareness motivates us to be more precise in formulating goals and strategies to reach our social justice ideals.

For some of us it may be a revelation that we are actually able to choose beliefs to guide our lives. All too often we experience ourselves as living according to others' beliefs, inheriting beliefs through several generations, and continuously meeting others' expectations. For example, we may feel obligated to sustain particular beliefs because they demonstrate loyalties to gender, race, ethnicity, or religion. However, social intelligence reminds us that although we need beliefs to motivate us to act, we are in charge of what these beliefs are or could be.

Both social intelligence and social justice are beliefs that we can choose to nurture and use. Although people are socially intelligent without knowing what social intelligence is, or may yearn for social justice without being aware of what social justice is, we can also educate ourselves about the many complexities of social intelligence and social justice, so that we get better positioned to strengthen these particular beliefs through our daily actions. Making investigative research commitments to understand both social intelligence and social justice helps us to use social intelligence and social justice to guide our behavior, so that we bring social intelligence and social justice to bear on our everyday choices.

Even though believing in both social intelligence and social justice does not immediately guarantee that we achieve them through our actions, when we choose to turn and move in these directions we gradually accomplish social intelligence and social justice goals. In fact, unless we believe in social intelligence and social justice, our well-intentioned endeavors to increase the common good may not be fruitful, because we may not be sufficiently prepared to deal with others' negative reactions to our initiatives to make constructive individual and social changes.

However, we need to pay attention to all our beliefs, in order to choose freely which beliefs we want to nurture and actualize in our exchanges with others. For example, we must reflect on our beliefs sufficiently to decide which beliefs contradict each other, and which beliefs help us to reach our social justice goals more effectively. When we explore what it means to believe in social intelligence, we use beliefs which are closely related to social intelligence, such as beliefs in the broad perspectives of objectivity; beliefs in our missions as historical actors; and beliefs in the importance of being responsible in our actions and commitments.

Social intelligence helps us to coordinate beliefs that inspire our choices to create social justice. For example, we examine our family beliefs so that we let go of unproductive beliefs and emphasize constructive beliefs. Starting with our family beliefs, we use objective views of our beliefs to decide which beliefs serve us best, in order to move in socially intelligent directions toward social justice. We also go outside our families to select beliefs that serve us well in our orientations as historical actors, and at the same time try to understand others' reactions to our contrasting beliefs. Moreover, when we make choices about our family beliefs, we recognize that these are only our choices. Consequently, we are sufficiently free to encourage others to decide which family beliefs they choose to guide themselves.

We also need to edit our beliefs about social classes, cultures, and societies because we realize the power and complexities of these diverse beliefs, as well as their consequences. Nevertheless, we have to agree that, as with our family beliefs, each of us is free to cultivate and use our own beliefs about social classes, cultures, and societies.

Modifying our beliefs, such as our family beliefs, deep-seated personal beliefs, social class beliefs, cultural beliefs, and societal beliefs, makes us more socially intelligent. By eliminating beliefs that conflict with each other, or cancel each other out, we clarify our priorities, and aim to express social justice ideals more effectively. By making it possible for others to have this same freedom of choice, we strengthen social intelligence and social justice in diverse social settings.

Socially Intelligent Choices and Social Classes

We examine how social intelligence creates social justice when we focus on social classes, because social classes permeate our actions in families, beliefs, cultures, and societies. Social classes, which are another of the five major social influences that make up our social intelligence, call into question our understanding of many social issues and concerns. Consequently, it is important to understand social classes as fully as possible, because social classes are central to social intelligence as well as social justice. However, before we can change social classes in order to increase social justice, we must recognize the overwhelming power of social classes, as well as their consequences for social behavior and social justice.

We often use historical records to track social class influences through time, as well as present trends in social classes in both traditional and modern societies. Although the occupants of particular social classes change in the long run, social hierarchies perpetuate themselves, with the result that members of upper social classes predictably continue to have considerably more advantages and life chances than members of lower social classes. Furthermore, even though education may make more opportunities available to members of lower social classes, gaps between the advantages of members of upper social classes and the resources of members of lower social classes often grow wider.

Besides being one of the five major social influences upon which social intelligence is built, social classes are at the core of all social inequalities in societies. Furthermore, social classes have many bases that need to be considered in making comparisons about their social consequences. For instance, social classes are hierarchies based on economic resources, material assets, social prestige, political power, education, occupations, ages, genders, sexual orientations, races, or ethnicities.

Social intelligence shows us that members of upper social classes consistently have bounteous resources and opportunities, whereas members of lower social classes have few resources and opportunities. Because upper and lower social classes in modern societies tend to have increasing rather than decreasing contrasts in resources, we need to be concerned about the perpetuation of social classes from generation to generation. Social intelligence helps us not only to understand social classes with wide ranges of social characteristics, but also to assess the different impacts of social classes on the qualities of life of their members from generation to generation.

Some socially intelligent strategies may ultimately reverse social processes that widen differences in life chances between members of upper and lower social classes. These strategies necessarily include designing alternative ways to organize societies. For example, social intelligence may inspire us to deny the power that social classes have to define our lives, and at the same time remind us about necessities to cooperate in work ventures rather than compete, so that we can achieve more equality and life-satisfaction in current societies.

These are some of the differences that social intelligence makes in neutralizing the overwhelming influence of social classes over significant areas of our lives. By shedding light on new choices about how we live each day in response to existing social classes, as well as possibilities for making new choices about social justice, social intelligence slowly but surely helps us to take control of some sources of social class inequalities.

In these respects, we find that social mobility no longer quiets our concerns about social class inequalities. In fact, we cannot merely direct our lives toward increasing social mobility, because successful social mobility maintains the status quo of social classes themselves, rather than assuages our socially intelligent concerns about the social well-being of all. However, once we value social intelligence, and work each day toward increasing social intelligence, we become more aware historical actors who make responsible commitments to embrace social justice values such as equality, inclusiveness, diversity, cooperation, and openness. In due course, the substance of making these different value choices diminishes the current hold that social class inequalities have over our collective well-being.

Social intelligence creates social justice in social classes because we act to modify how we organize our social lives around established social class hierarchies that reward a few and penalize many. For example, when we really want to increase the common good and social justice, we cannot stay ignorant about the perniciousness of social classes. Our responsibilities as historical actors ultimately include making sure that we eliminate as many unfair inequalities as possible, and replace mainstream value choices with alternative value choices, such as those for equality, inclusiveness, diversity, cooperation, and openness.

Socially Intelligent Choices and Cultures

Being clearly established in social intelligence, as well as socially intelligent choices about cultures, enhances possibilities for creating social justice through social intelligence. Cultures are another of the five major social influences of social intelligence which affect how populations establish their priorities and reach agreement about supporting or rejecting particular values. In these respects cultures often permeate our thinking and actions, because they predispose individuals and societies to accept or reject particular ways of communicating or transacting their day-to-day business.

Social intelligence helps us to see relationships between individuals' culture choices and social outcomes for whole societies and globalization. For example, we act with greater awareness about our cultural options when we are socially intelligent. Furthermore, to the extent that we see marked differences between constructive or destructive cultures, individually-oriented or collectively-oriented cultures, and life-enhancing or death-directed cultures, we are more discerning in the cultural and social choices we make each day. Being historical actors further increases our awareness of the impact of time on our value choices, so that we become more deliberately oriented to past, present, or future cultures through our socially intelligent choices.

These particular focuses and orientations of social intelligence prepare us to take enlightened social actions such as increasing social justice. Although people who are not aware of social intelligence accomplish many good works and increase social justice, they are successful in proceeding in these directions largely because of their astute observation, learning, and understanding of the nature of human nature. Deliberately studying social intelligence, by examining families, beliefs, social classes, cultures, and societies, is a tool that all can use to reach these same goals, as well as a tool which makes both random and concerted efforts to increase social justice more effective.

We know that we are on the right track to increase social justice when we are aware of the power and complexities of families, beliefs, social classes, cultures, and societies that assist or block opportunities and means for increasing social justice. We also recognize that we are on productive paths, when we see that our choices—in relation to families, beliefs, social classes, cultures, and societies—have increased beyond recognition. In addition, we respect cultures more in terms of their unending sources of inspiration with regard to choosing social justice goals, and choosing those particular values that will predispose us to build strong societal foundations and supports for social justice.

Some of the particular cultural values that create social conditions conducive to increasing social justice are equality, inclusiveness, diversity, cooperation, and openness. For example, when we try to treat others as equals in pursuing our goals, we honor universal characteristics of the human condition. In fact, we only truly respect individuals and populations when we pay adequate attention to others' needs as well as our own. Thus, caring about the well-being of all influences the choices we identify and make as we go about our everyday lives.

Similarly, the cultural choice of inclusiveness is a reminder that we should orient our good works, so that they reach all members of our populations rather than particular groups. For example, we cannot afford to have individuals or marginal groups excluded from the advantages of modern industrial societies, because we know that lifetimes are too short and resources too limited to consider this a satisfactory situation. Furthermore, only when people choose to meet the needs of all can we live responsibly in thriving societies.

Diversity is another cultural choice, which takes us closer to realizing overall satisfactory social conditions. We discover that it is not feasible merely to cling to familiar relationships or vested interests without caring about the rest of the world. Globalization makes diversity a widespread social reality, and we must embrace diversity in populations through honoring rich varieties in cultures that reflect vital human possibilities and accomplishments. We also need to pay debts to those who have been exploited in the past, to ensure that all can enjoy present and future societies.

The cultural choice of cooperation challenges the more usual cultural choices of competition. In critical respects, when we aim to cooperate with others we essentially override past choices to compete, so that we learn more about what it takes to work collectively toward social justice goals. Even though being sufficiently socially intelligent to cooperate with others is not yet a widespread social reality, we already see some of the positive impacts that cooperation has on our children and peers. This progress is sufficient to inspire us to continue to hone our skills to cooperate with others now and in the future.

Finally, we honor cultural choices which lead us to be honest and transparent in our motives and goals, by choosing to be open in how we conduct our business and personal exchanges with others in the present. In contrast to past secret, sometimes underhand ways of achieving our goals and manipulating others, we make clearer cultural choices that are open to others' consideration and scrutiny, as well as initiate new value choices that further develop social justice in and among our societies.

Socially Intelligent Choices and Societies

Choices in societies are often not readily apparent. For example, there are many life stages—especially when we are very young or very old—when we have fewer real or imagined choices because of our more acute dependence on others. It is only when adult children gain their independence that they experience relatively free choices about how they want to spend their lives. For example, cutting some ties with our parents, or powerful others, helps us to recognize choices that lie beyond our basic dependency needs.

Our choices as adults range from personal choices about our families and beliefs, to more public choices about social classes, cultures, and societies. Our broadest social intelligence perspectives flow from our positions in societies, which require us to see as many choices as possible from our varied vantage points. Furthermore, because all societies are affected by globalization, considering the world at large as sources of choices expands our horizons and multiplies our options. We are citizens of the world, as well as citizens of our nation states, and as socially intelligent agents of history we need to consider broad interdependency issues among and between societies as well as within societies.

When the contours of our social landscapes change, we can make more enlightened choices about social justice. Social intelligence opens up new knowledge and awareness about our social embeddedness, so that we are better equipped to understand the significance of social justice, and respond to vocations that summon us to be responsible in local, national, and global contexts. We also seek to understand and interact with the five major social influences of families, beliefs, social classes, cultures, and societies, in order to be more objective, as well as more fully prepared to increase social intelligence, the common good, and social justice.

Examining societies from points of view of the past, present, and future frees us to use ever-broadening perspectives to establish our priorities and societal goals. We become parts of societies and globalization when we formulate national and international goals to meet the universal needs of populations. Socially intelligent broad commitments accomplish useful goals that try to address universal needs within, between, and among societies in globalization. In fact, merely by changing the scope of our concerns from local to global populations, we create broader universes of individual and societal choices.

Valuing equality, inclusiveness, and diversity enriches the qualities of our existing societies, so that we achieve more integrated social networks in present societies than in the past. These prepare us today for the future, so that we work together more productively to make real progress in accomplishing social justice concerns. By committing ourselves to be historical actors, we work with like-minded others whenever possible, in order to cooperate more effectively by opening up difficult social issues and closed personal, social, and political relationships. Understanding which social or emotional systems drive our societies makes us alert to the many advantages of socially intelligent actions which lead to social justice.

Societies consistently give us useful perspectives for understanding our families, beliefs, social classes, and cultures. For example, when societies are at war, we think and act dramatically differently from usual in our families, beliefs, social classes, and cultures. Wartime makes us more collectively-oriented, so that we tend to be more patriotic in our thinking and acting. Our families help us to cope with the privations of war, especially if some of our strongest family members are exposed to life-threatening circumstances on a daily basis. We also discover that we need social justice beliefs to help us to understand some of the atrocious social conditions and cruelties of war. Sometimes our beliefs are so strongly tested by societies' war situations, that we feel pressured to change deep-seated beliefs that we previously took for granted.

Even social classes lose many of their meanings in wartime. For example, we are less motivated to be socially mobile because the stakes of everyday life are completely different from those in times of peace and prosperity. However, we may also choose to care for people with the most obvious needs amidst warfare, or to honor the fact that disproportionate numbers of lives are lost among members of lower social classes. In some respects, our increased empathy for members of lower social classes in wartime may change cultures in the present and future, because stressful wartimes create more practical, egalitarian exchanges between wealthier and poorer members of our populations. Consequently, more people may choose to work directly for social justice in wartime than during periods of peace and prosperity.

Socially Intelligent Choices, Social Intelligence, and Social Justice

Socially intelligent choices move us toward social justice by increasing the common good. Subsequently, we persist in making socially intelligent choices, because these open up more social justice possibilities.

Being socially intelligent, aware, and responsible requires us to continue making socially intelligent choices toward social justice, as long as we think that we are on the right track to accomplish social justice goals. Social intelligence is a tool that helps us to achieve social justice, and a tool that shows us how to accomplish social justice goals. Whereas previously we may have understood very little about social justice, social intelligence makes us more knowledgeable about social justice issues and situations.

Social intelligence consistently serves us as a means of understanding, which guides us to make thoughtful choices. Social intelligence is also a reservoir of information about societies that leads us toward greater personal fulfillment, as well as to the attainment of social justice goals. Even when we reach impasses in how to make social justice changes, we can still be inspired by socially intelligent wisdom and enlightenment, so that we try new ways to accomplish our well-thought-out objectives. Social intelligence is a dependable resource for accomplishing whatever we do, and for whatever outcomes we have in achieving social justice.

When we align our daily socially intelligent choices with our social intelligence capacities, we can be confident that we are moving in productive directions. These pointers allow us to increase our attention to social justice issues, so that we are prompted to re-examine our social circumstances and choices whenever necessary. We cultivate habits of scrutinizing our thoughts and actions, so that we become more committed to our social justice goals and the socially intelligent means we choose, as well as to cooperating with likeminded others to create our preferred future societies.

Social intelligence creates social justice by illuminating our actions about families. Although it is important to understand our own families, and interact with our relatives in socially intelligent ways, we cannot aspire to merely participate differently in our own families. In order to be socially intelligent, and to realize social justice in relation to families, we must see families from broader perspectives of beliefs, social classes, cultures, and societies. Only then do we discern significant relationships between social intelligence and social justice.

In addition, we need to continuously examine our beliefs, social classes, cultures, and societies from the points of view of our available choices. We maintain objectivity and broad views of social justice by seeing more choices in how to interact with beliefs, social classes, cultures, and societies. For example, we are stronger historical actors when we cultivate well-integrated beliefs, freedom from social class pressures, clear senses of meaning and purpose about cultural values, and awareness of societies' varied opportunities.

Being thoughtful about interrelationships among families, beliefs, social classes, cultures, and societies provides us with new daily choices and new goals for accomplishing social justice. We think in terms of social systems and value choices when we use social intelligence to pursue social justice goals, which strengthen and enlighten our day-by-day endeavors. For example, our knowledge of social systems helps us to appreciate how the consequences of our actions are both wanted and unwanted, so that we take responsibility for all these outcomes, in order to be more successful in our social justice endeavors.

Thus the primary reason to be concerned about the socially intelligent dimensions of our choices is to increase our odds for success in accomplishing social justice changes. The preparations we make in fine tuning our choices pay off in terms of securing firmer successes in pursuing our chosen social justice goals. Consequently, when we try to be socially intelligent, and persist in making socially intelligent choices, we do more of what we really want to accomplish with our lives. We second guess ourselves less, and at the same time make deeper commitments to share responsibilities with others to achieve complex social justice goals.

XII. Socially Intelligent Changes and Social Justice

Socially intelligent changes educate us sufficiently to see the many benefits of trying to increase social justice. For example, we realize that we cannot live fully if we stop developing our social intelligence, because the world is bigger than our knowledge of how societies work. Furthermore, we are increasingly motivated to find ways to express our social intelligence through social justice.

Socially intelligent changes create new syntheses of social justice. Although we cannot arrive at all the changes we need to strengthen social justice now, we make improvements in social justice through incremental socially intelligent changes in ourselves, our communities, and our populations. This is not to say that socially intelligent changes cannot be substantial, but that we should not expect more than gradual changes from socially intelligent strategies most of the time.

Because our social intelligence depends on our working knowledge of families, beliefs, social classes, cultures, and societies, we must pay particular attention to those socially intelligent changes we can make in families that increase social justice in societies. For example, socializing our children to accept adult responsibilities for themselves and others leads to social justice benefits in both families and societies.

Similarly, we want to be sure that the beliefs we entertain and nurture express motives and goals which bring about socially intelligent changes, rather than disjointed or conflicting compromises that cannot strengthen social justice in our societies. We persist in increasing our social intelligence about beliefs in our families, social classes, cultures, and societies so that we can be more socially intelligent in using our beliefs to develop the common good and social justice. For example, we may examine our religious beliefs to ensure that they are consistent with how we conduct our lives and make our daily choices, so that our beliefs have more constructive impacts on our successes in social justice ventures.

Our awareness of the power and complexities of social classes makes us more socially intelligent about initiating particular social class changes in our lives and societies. For example, we are more discerning about the limits of our influences on what we do and what we accomplish in social justice, when we are objective and socially intelligent in our choices of interventions in social classes. Above all, we need to maintain our understanding of the importance of making socially intelligent changes about social classes to increase social justice, because social class inequalities limit whole populations.

At the same time that we increase our social intelligence, we see the beneficial effects of changing our cultures and value choices. Even though using the socially intelligent values of equality, inclusiveness, diversity, cooperation, and openness may not guarantee increased social justice in societies, we can accomplish slow progress in establishing cultural conditions that are conducive to nurturing social justice when we make such new value choices. Changing our emphases and ways of doing things helps us to create innovative social practices, as well as different ways to conduct our day-to-day business both within and between societies.

Societies give us the broadest perspectives from which to assess our social intelligence and the changes we make to increase social intelligence and social justice. When we consider these broadest contexts of the power and complexities of families, beliefs, social classes, cultures, and societies, we understand the strength of our tendencies to merely repeat the status quo of our social arrangements and social interactions. Nevertheless, making deliberate use of social intelligence to change social problems neutralizes automatic behaviors which otherwise would only extend or react to the past. For example, we are more responsible historical actors when we give priority to the present and future, by designing new social realities that are built on social justice.

We expect social intelligence to guide us in making useful changes in societies now for the future, and realize that as long as we are headed in this direction, social justice will be stronger in the next generations. Although our results and aspirations may be vague, optimism can carry us toward improving our lives through using the social justice values of equality, inclusiveness, diversity, cooperation, and openness. Furthermore, social justice ideals do not die, which makes it practical to use them to guide our actions in our regular routines, as well as in critical times of destruction, anguish and despair.

Socially Intelligent Changes and Families

Social intelligence often appears to err on the side of not making sufficient changes in families, although this view essentially expresses some people's negative reactions to social intelligence principles. For example, social intelligence emphasizes the critical importance of making gradual changes in established patterns of family dominance. These interventions aim to rectify imbalances in family leadership, so that each family member gains more freedom to come and go in relation to varied family pressures. Furthermore, such a socially intelligent strategy shows that slight changes in what families do, are usually more widely accepted than radical proposals to undo several generations' ways of managing family stability and responsibilities.

In the long run, accumulations of small socially intelligent changes increase social justice in family relations, and may ultimately create major differences in how family members care for themselves and others around survival and fulfillment concerns. This approach to making socially intelligent changes is meaningful, because it challenges even one family member to accomplish socially intelligent changes, as well as several family members. Given these odds, any person introducing socially intelligent changes becomes a new kind of family leader whom others may choose to follow or not.

Socially intelligent family changes do not necessarily include some of the more radical and extreme changes found in many modern families. For example, social intelligence often prompts us to think through more fully whether or not to get or stay married, and whether or not to be in touch with difficult-to-get-along-with family members. More important, from the point of view of social intelligence, is to emphasize the significance of building firm family foundations for ourselves and others in our current family networks. Thus, our families' emotional systems may be committed to try many ways to sustain our family bonds rather than sever them. In this vein, social intelligence also cultivates flexible family relationships, rather than tolerates tight or rigid family bonds that do not allow a free give and take among relatives in the same families.

Merely getting to know more about who's who among our past and current family members is an effective socially intelligent way to anchor our identities in our family networks. For example, we create and enhance our identities more deliberately when we forge meaningful relationships with members of our extended families. These contacts open up some of the brittle restrictiveness of our most familiar nuclear family bonds. Furthermore, when we collect social facts about our extended family members, we create family histories that give us more clues about who we could be, what we could choose to do with our lives, and how we can create strong but flexible ties with our relatives.

Being well-integrated with our families, and being free to go out into the world away from our families, opens up our family relationships, so that we think more clearly about which socially intelligent family changes need to be made for the good of all. We apply the social intelligence principle of universal care, by first considering what our own families need. After taking responsible action to meet our families' real needs, we turn more knowledgeably toward considering the needs of other families in our societies and abroad.

Because of the emotional system qualities of our families, we learn not only about social justice from our families, but also about their resistance to social justice. This socially intelligent knowledge and skill is later transferred to other groups of various sources and sizes, as well as to historically significant social processes such as conflicts, losses, and globalization. For example, families show us that human behavior is volatile because it is emotional, and that families demonstrate some of the many ways in which emotional pressures among people are expressed and released through patterns of family interaction.

Social intelligence gives us some control over our actions by educating us about family changes, and the significance of interdependence in our overall behavior and relationships. For example, when we are less dependent on others in our families, we are more socially intelligent within our families and in other social settings. Being sufficiently free and objective in our views of social situations, decisions, and commitments increases our capacities to believe in social justice, to decide to increase social justice, and to make commitments with others to achieve social justice goals.

In these respects, we benefit from maintaining our families as foundations and launching pads for our social justice work as historical actors. We use our working knowledge of families as guiding principles of social intelligence, so that we are more capable historical actors in pursuing social justice goals. Consequently, we bring social justice into our families and other social settings, so that we can work to establish stronger societies built on social justice.

Socially Intelligent Changes and Beliefs

Incremental social intelligence changes may also transform our beliefs. By comparing our most cherished beliefs with social facts and social realities, we get a reliable sense of how far our beliefs may be from actual social situations, and whether or not our beliefs are too unrealistic to guide us in our everyday lives. When we question the usefulness of our beliefs, and are critical about the success of our beliefs in supporting our goals to make socially intelligent or social justice changes, we at the same time fruitfully assess how we need to modify them.

This testing of our beliefs, and the results of our beliefs, is also a process of enlightenment, which guides our understanding of social realities and social facts, as well as our motives to be socially intelligent or to increase social justice. If our beliefs do not stand up to our scrutiny of their usefulness and effectiveness, social intelligence suggests that we should turn to new values to motivate us to accomplish the common good or social justice. For example, we may aim to increase equality, inclusiveness, diversity, cooperation, and openness in our everyday exchanges with others, so that we make more social conditions conducive to establishing social justice.

We continue to scrutinize our beliefs for a lifetime, which means that our work in major social spheres is never complete. This is a positive challenge, because it wakens us to the power and complexities of the social realities we need to modify through time. However, unless we have a sufficiently clear socially intelligent awareness, we will continue to perpetuate contradictory or ineffective beliefs in our families, social classes, cultures, and societies. By contrast, our awareness of these behavior patterns and needs in current social conditions increases our social intelligence, and prepares us to make more effective increases in social justice.

When we examine our beliefs about families, we see that much of what we believe is a complex mix of the opinions of relatives, especially those of our parents. When we are young and impressionable, we absorb beliefs uncritically, reinforcing emotional patterns of closeness and dominance among our relatives, that often determine what we eventually believe. Sometimes it seems to be an impossibly daunting challenge to reverse or modify our earliest family beliefs, because these beliefs seep into our deepest levels of being, and are often taken for granted, rather than recognized as influences on our behavior that should be changed.

Our beliefs about social classes, which are also produced by strong family influences, may be equally intransigent. We initially absorb much information about social classes, such as social emphases that show us what and how social classes are, without developing any particular questions about the social realities or necessities of social classes. However, when we mature and experiment with expanding our social intelligence, we may become more convinced that the social facts and social realities expressed by social classes can be changed and improved. For example, our interest in social justice often grows precisely because we want social classes to be different. Consequently, by imagining alternatives to existing social classes, historical actors may believe that non-hierarchical options can be used to organize populations, in order to realize social justice conditions of equality, inclusiveness, diversity, cooperation, and openness.

Similarly, when we turn to cultures and societies to assess the usefulness of our current beliefs, we find rich varieties of alternatives to the social facts and social realities that we experience daily in our cultures. By fine-tuning our beliefs to envision new social justice goals, we aim more accurately to increase social justice, especially when we incorporate new values into our beliefs individually and socially. For example, we increase social justice by implementing values of equality, inclusiveness, diversity, cooperation, and openness in whatever we do individually, and with those with whom we work.

These are some of the most vital socially intelligent changes we can make in our beliefs, so that we become more active in building social justice. Our social intelligence ensures that we stay on track to accomplish social justice goals, and we continue to increase our social intelligence as we express social justice in our actions. The span of concerns affected by changing our beliefs cuts across past, present, and future times, and focuses on personal, family, community, and national or international agendas.

Socially Intelligent Changes and Social Classes

Both social intelligence and social justice inevitably lead to changing social conditions we may have taken for granted. Focusing on making individual or social changes requires caution and responsibility, because social strategies may have harmful consequences in addition to beneficial results. However well-planned we think we are at intervening in business as usual, we must be ready to deal with the unexpected effects of our well-intentioned actions.

Nowhere are social intelligence principles more self-evident than when we make changing social classes an individual and collective goal. Using social intelligence to understand social classes is often considered a personal endeavor, because the social consequences of individuals making different choices about social classes affect interpersonal commitments more directly than social conditions in societies. However, ultimately we need to become sufficiently concerned about the social consequences of social classes, in order to formulate collective social justice goals for social class changes.

Using social intelligence to create alternatives to social classes may start to transform societies as well as individual lives. For example, when we work with socially intelligent historical actors, we usually seek to actively encourage more responsible alternative value choices—such as, equality, inclusiveness, diversity, cooperation, and openness—that make social conditions in societies qualitatively different from our current traditional or modern social class hierarchies.

The initiation of socially intelligent changes in social classes is largely a thoughtful response to social facts and social realities that define contrasts in the advantages and disadvantages of population members who are in upper and lower social classes. The increasing gap between upper and lower social class privileges in modern societies is troubling, because we have not yet found acceptable ways to control these contrasts, in spite of the spread of mass education throughout the populations of many contemporary societies. However, even though our socially intelligent goals do not necessarily achieve equality in current conditions, there is no doubt that moving in a direction of the social ideal of social justice makes appreciable improvements to existing inequalities.

Given these social facts and social realities, social intelligence draws our attention to the principle that increasing the social mobility of individuals is not the same goal as increasing equality, which is accomplished by making the benefits of resources in today's societies more accessible. Furthermore, wherever traditional social class hierarchies persist, widespread experiences of relative deprivation cancel out some of the increased freedom we may gain from social mobility.

Rather, we need to clarify our plans to cooperate to create new designs that increase the common good and social justice for all. This is a tall order that requires feasible strategies. Moreover, just because societies have not yet accomplished such radical changes, we cannot give up trying to design worthwhile goals that organize populations differently, especially when our survival depends on creating social conditions that will sustain peaceful co-existence both within and among societies.

A mission to explore alternative ways to organize populations ensures that we can begin to make substantial revisions in how we live in relation to social classes. A socially intelligent approach to solving social justice issues of inequalities in social classes may also inspire new ways to raise and educate our children. For example, it is possible to create more freedom for children to interact differently with their peers, so that we can aspire to goals that encourage societies to work more effectively by producing basic goods and services for all. This is accomplished not through manipulative social engineering, but rather as dividends of cooperative collaborations that clarify and achieve dependable social ideals, such as the common good and social justice.

Knowing that socially intelligent social class changes would eventually improve societies is heartening, and encourages our further attention to plan for social justice as individuals and co-workers. Social intelligence makes us focus on the larger picture of our well-being, which serves as continuing inspiration to accomplish the common good and social justice. We find that when we are prepared to deal with social facts and social realities, our social justice efforts endure more into the future than when we act solely according to our intuitions and feelings. This is so because socially intelligent resolutions of social class issues depend more on our clear thoughts than on our yearnings to feel good about our social positions in society.

Socially Intelligent Changes and Cultures

Cultures are another of the five major social influences that make up our social intelligence and our ways of understanding social facts and social realities. As well as families, beliefs, social classes, and societies, cultures yield resources that propel our socially intelligent changes to increase the common good and social justice. This dynamic power of cultures exists because cultures are made up of miscellaneous values, ideals, norms, knowledge, laws, religions, dreams, sciences, technologies, and other aspects of how we become human and stay humane in our dealings with each other. Consequently, we depend on cultures to motivate us and define our senses of meaning, purpose, and direction. This momentum suggests that cultures are, and will continue to be, essential social influences in our past, present, and future worlds.

In order to sort out some of the critical mass of our vast cultures and their varied impacts on our everyday lives, it is sometimes useful to make distinctions among the many values that make up our cultures. For example, we benefit from distinguishing constructive cultures from destructive cultures, individually-oriented cultures from collectively-oriented cultures, and life-enhancing cultures from death-directed cultures. In line with the positive contributions of social intelligence emphasized in *Social Intelligence and Social Justice*, many readers and population members are interested in maintaining cultures that are constructive, collectively-oriented, and life-enhancing, thereby avoiding cultures that are destructive, individually-oriented, and death-directed.

These culture categories help us to sort out which values we need to use to make socially intelligent changes in our cultures, so that we accomplish social justice. For example, we benefit from becoming more precise in our preferences for social justice values—such as equality, inclusiveness, diversity, cooperation, and openness—in our cultures. Thus, expanding the common good, through socially intelligent changes, increases the likelihood that we will be effective in achieving social justice in our cultures and societies.

Our cultures continue to motivate us and refresh our minds about these possibilities. When we believe we are stuck in our efforts to increase social justice, for example, we routinely find new ideas and values to orient our actions through reviewing varied cultures. Because we are focused on social intelligence when we make our everyday value choices, we discover that we are more effective historical actors when we understand history through our cultures and habitual value choices. Also, we are better prepared to explore new territories by making new value choices, because constructive value choices are foundations for creating improved cultural and social conditions.

Cultures are dependable resources that enlighten and support our socially intelligent changes. We are able to approach social justice because we respect the many different dimensions of cultures that influence our daily choices and changes: for example, family cultures, cultures of beliefs, social class cultures, and historical societal cultures. Moreover, when we recognize the power and complexities of cultures in whatever we do, we are more successful in accomplishing socially intelligent changes in cultures and social justice.

In order to be convinced that some of these individual and social change possibilities move us toward social justice, we try to test social intelligence principles in our everyday lives.

For example, it is relatively easy to check the pervasiveness of our cultures, as well as the different cultural values that have assumed the most historical importance in our lives, due to the influences of our families and relatives. Why do we repeat our behavior when we know that this may be counterproductive? On whom do we depend for spiritual or secular guidance in our lives? Do the clusters of values in the religious or secular beliefs we were raised with still influence how we think and what we do?

We re-educate ourselves through increasing our social intelligence, and we discover many ways to strengthen the meaningfulness of our lives by making socially intelligent value choices. This frees us to give more attention to social justice issues that may have concerned us over a lifetime. Can we find ways to relate to our cultures more objectively, so that we are prepared to carve out more meaningful cultural directions? Can we change directions in our decisions and value commitments where necessary? How does social justice touch our lives? Can we find more universal ways to make socially intelligent changes, so that we are not sole beneficiaries of our cultural work to increase the common good?

Socially Intelligent Changes and Societies

It is difficult to know how to aim for social justice, and how to achieve social justice changes, without having reliable ways and means to assess what is going on in societies at large. This overview helps us to discern what we could do to make viable social changes. All too often we cherish overly optimistic images of what we think societies are or should be, but such distortions of social realities are not productive. We need to be as objective and realistic as possible, so that we approach social issues from universalistic viewpoints, if we are to make progress in improving social justice and the quality of life for all.

Societies are one of the five most significant social influences that make up our understanding of the power and complexities of social forces and social intelligence. Societies are also our broadest perspectives on social realities. We can only make substantial changes in how we interact with others in the context of our societies, that is when we understand the major patterns in widespread interactions that have persisted through time. For example, seeing gender roles within societies' power relations makes us more aware of the social forces that resist gender changes, as well as the social pressures that support the social justice value of equality between genders.

Considering societies focuses our attention particularly on the parts that social influences play in history and historical changes. When we increase our social intelligence, we gain some control over historical changes, and consequently are more likely to strive to be observant and responsible historical actors who work to achieve social justice goals. The more we increase our social intelligence through these endeavors, the more we make wise choices that expand and create social justice. Both our individual and collective efforts to be responsible historical actors move us forward in these constructive directions.

Although it is important to understand our families and social justice changes from the perspectives of our families, we also need to view trends and patterns in family behavior throughout our societies and in the international community, so that we can see the power and complexities of these influences and their impacts on social justice. Similarly, we strive to recognize social complexities in our experiences of beliefs, social classes, and cultures, as well as from broad societal perspectives on social changes, especially in areas that affect our value choices in the present for the future. Our views of these social realities deepen our knowledge of societies, and help us to make more strategic interventions to accomplish social justice changes.

The broadest view of our societies and societal changes is an evolutionary perspective. This panoramic view of societies through time is difficult to comprehend, especially in its details, but it usefully requires us to take a step back in assessing socially intelligent choices about changing societies, so that we consider the nature of human nature, as well as possibilities and limits in realistic changes for social justice. Whatever our assumptions are about social realities— those related to either natural or sacred universes—they have considerable impacts on our social intelligence, our understanding of the common good, and our capacities to achieve social justice.

In addition to knowing the histories of societies, we must be sufficiently immersed in the present to assess current trends in globalization and international communities. Although economic resources appear to dominate relations between powerful and less powerful countries, cultural traditions must also be taken into account in realizing the extent to which societies need social justice changes that increase opportunities and access to social resources for all. Social intelligence is a useful guide for understanding world changes as they happen, as well as for planning interventions that move us into better futures. In this respect we honor the histories of our societies, as well as their current situations and future possibilities.

When we consider societies, evolution, and globalization, social intelligence is at the cutting edge of informed social changes toward social justice. For example, social intelligence is a dependable resource for planning future-oriented social changes of varied dimensions. Social intelligence also has important implications for individuals who increase their social intelligence in order to be responsible historical actors. Only when individuals are sufficiently aware of the complex social contexts in which they live, can they initiate enlightened actions that build social justice in the present for better futures. Consequently, when we move into broad spheres of societal changes, we use social intelligence to ensure that our actions increase social justice effectively.

Socially Intelligent Changes, Social Intelligence, and Social Justice

When we look at linkages among socially intelligent changes, social intelligence, and social justice, we need to be vigilant about how our behavior is predictably affected by both personal relationships and broad social forces. For example, we are too passive if we claim that we need to wait for a spiritual calling or a religious vocation to direct us to pursue social justice. Although such revelations may come through either religious or secular beliefs, it is imperative that we use all our thinking capacities now, as resources to increase our socially intelligent awareness and knowledge, so that we can act toward accomplishing feasible social justice goals and changes.

Social intelligence often enlightens us in the early stages of our journeys toward taking action to increase social justice. We may not respond exclusively to our senses of moral purpose, but rather seek to do the most practical thing in ambiguous situations, given the power and complexities of our social experiences in families, beliefs, social classes, cultures, and societies.

We also increase our awareness of the pervasiveness and dominance of these five major social influences, so that we see more clearly that we are responsible for our destinies. Thus, the outcomes of our futures lie at least partly in our own hands.

Even though our influences over the social forces of families, beliefs, social classes, cultures, and societies are limited, we can make some enlightened and effective social changes to increase social justice. Furthermore, our socially intelligent changes predictably make considerable differences to the well-being of those who are currently disadvantaged.

We decide to proceed slowly toward social justice because this goal answers our concerns about what we need to do to change the strong tides of limited social realities that perpetuate the status quo of our current societies. We see that innovative value choices—such as equality, inclusiveness, diversity, cooperation, and openness—impact our emotionally fraught social relations, as well as those much-desired social resources that drive self-interested behavior in contemporary industrialized societies. Thus, social justice offers workable options for peaceful co-existence, which are often our only viable recourse in a dangerous and volatile world. When we are consistently deliberate in our quests to increase our social intelligence, we strengthen interests in social justice, so that we gradually make more meaningful commitments to work alone or with others to accomplish social justice changes.

In these respects, social intelligence is part of the process that enables us to approach and accomplish social justice goals. Socially intelligent means support our quests to increase the common good and social justice, so that more people have access to social resources in our societies and throughout the world. Moreover, we focus on the timing of our social interventions so that we increase their effectiveness, and continue to work toward social justice goals in spite of many setbacks or insufficient courage. Social intelligence refreshes our efforts to keep going in spite of others' resistance to innovations that increase social justice.

Because social intelligence is often built on expectations that we will use our heightened awareness to engage in socially useful actions, tensions between this awareness and social facts continue to motivate us to close gaps in contrasting advantages between members of upper and lower social classes. For example, we may work hard to make education more available to disadvantaged groups, because this change ensures that more people throughout populations read and write fluently. Even though education may seem fairly remote from our socially intelligent goal to reduce inequalities across social classes, in the long run such broad social changes can be accomplished.

Being aware, responsible historical actors allows us to tune in to a variety of current needs in our societies. Social intelligence directs us toward changes that seem practical to accomplish, given our particular social skills and social resources. Thus, we come full circle in creating legacies from social justice changes that we were able to achieve through applying social intelligence principles and social justice ideals. Furthermore, social justice increases our fulfillment, because we realize that others benefit from our socially intelligent choices and changes, as well as ourselves. Consequently, we trust that societies will gradually accept the social justice value choices of equality, inclusiveness, diversity, cooperation, and openness more fully, as foundations for peaceful co-existence.

Suggested Reading

Anderson, Elijah. 1999. *Code of the Street: Decency, Violence, and the Moral Life of the Inner City.* New York: W. W. Norton.

Arana, Marie. 2001. *American Chica: Two Worlds, One Childhood.* New York: Random House.

Barber, Benjamin R. 1995. *Jihad vs. McWorld: How Globalism and Tribalism Are Reshaping the World.* New York: Random House.

Best, Joel. 2004. *More Damned Lies and Statistics: How Numbers Confuse Public Issues,* 2nd ed. Berkeley, CA: University of California Press.

Chang, Grace. 2000. *Disposable Domestics: Immigrant Women Workers in the Global Economy.* Boston, MA: South End Press.

Craig, Gary, Tania Burchardt, and David Gordon. 2008. *Social Justice and Public Policy: Seeking Fairness in Diverse Societies.* Bristol, UK: The Policy Press.

Domhoff, G. William. 1998. *Who Rules America?* Mountain View, CA: Mayfield Publishing.

Du Bois, W. E. B. 1994/1903. *The Souls of Black Folk.* New York: Dover Publications.

Ehrenreich, Barbara. 2001. *Nickel and Dimed: On (Not) Getting By in America.* New York: Metropolitan Books.

Freeman, Jo. 1999. *Waves of Protest: Social Movements Since the Sixties.* Lanham, MD: Rowman and Littlefield.

Gans, Herbert J. 1999. *Popular Culture and High Culture: An Analysis and Evaluation of Taste.* New York: Basic Books.

Gittlin, Todd. 2002. *Media Unlimited: How the Torrent of Images and Sounds Overwhelms Our Lives.* New York: Metropolitan Books.

Kanter, Rosabeth Moss. 1977. *Men and Women of the Corporation.* New York: Basic Books.

Kilbourne, Jean. 1999. *Can't Buy my Love: How Advertising Changes the Way We Think and Feel.* New York: Simon and Schuster. Martinez, Ramiro. 2002. *Latino Homicide: Immigration, Violence and Community.* New York: Routledge.

Mauer, Marc. 1999. *Race to Incarcerate.* New York: The New Press.

Mills, C. Wright. 1959. *The Sociological Imagination.* New York: Oxford University Press.

Putnam, Robert D. 2000. *Bowling Alone: The Collapse and Revival of American Community.* New York: Simon and Schuster.

Reiman, Jeffrey. 2004. *The Rich Get Richer and the Poor Get Prison?* 7th ed. Boston, MA: Allyn and Bacon.

Ritzer, George. 2002. *The McDonaldization of Society: An Investigation Into the Changing Character of Contemporary Society and Life*, 2nd ed. Newbury Park, CA: Pine Forge Press.

Schlosser, Eric. 2001. *Fast Food Nation: The Dark Side of the All-American Meal.* New York: Houghton Mifflin.

Schneider, Barbara, and David Stevenson. 1999. *The Ambitious Generation: America's Teenagers, Motivated but Directionless.* New Haven: Yale University Press.

Wilson, William Julius. 1996. *When Work Disappears.* Chicago, IL: University of Chicago Press.

With many thanks to my colleagues at Georgetown University Sociology Department, the Bowen Center for the Study of the Family, the Association for Applied and Clinical Sociology, and the International Sociological Association (Research Committee 46, Clinical Sociology). I am also indebted to my clients and students, who have taught me so much, and to my wonderful American and English families, who continue to stand by me on a daily basis.